The Spark in the Soul

The Spark in the Soul

Spirituality and Social Justice

TERRY TASTARD

Foreword by
Michael Hollings

Darton Longman and Todd
London

First published in 1989 by
Darton, Longman and Todd Ltd
89 Lillie Road, London SW6 1UD

© 1989 Terry Tastard SSF

British Library Cataloguing in Publication Data

Tastard, Terry
  The spark in the soul.
  1. Christian life. Spirituality. History
  I. Title
  248.4'09

ISBN 0–232–51797–5

Phototypeset by
Input Typesetting Ltd, London
Printed and Bound in Great Britain by
Courier International Ltd, Tiptree, Essex

To my mother
Jessie Niven Tastard
and in memory of my father
David Hunter Tastard

Contents

Foreword

Put crudely, traditional Christian teaching on the spiritual life has polarized between fleeing from the world to find God in solitude and silence, and immersing oneself in the world in order to find God in people and service. A superficial and inaccurate understanding of the relationship of God, mankind and the world tends to separate these two ways almost completely – suggesting that contemplative prayer is the prerogative of the monk or nun shut away from the distraction of active life in the world.

As a city-based priest and one who was first led towards ordination by a desire to be working for people, the contrast and lack of balance which can be nurtured from this acceptance of an either/or alternative way of life has struck me forcibly in this way. Thirty odd years ago, I stayed some days in a Carthusian monastery, attending Vespers each evening. One by one the monks came in, each pulling the bell rope in the centre of the church before going to their place in choir, until all were assembled and the office began. Twenty years later, I was again staying nearby and made a point of going to Vespers. During those years, I had been in five different appointments, travelled and worked widely through the world, and regularly depended as much or more upon my own energy as on God's power. And all that time, monks had been faithfully tolling the bell each day within the monastery enclosure. I was reminded of Gerard Manley Hopkins' poem:

> Yet God (that hews mountain and continent
> Earth, all, out; who, with trickling increment,

Veins violets and tall trees makes more and more)
Could crowd career with conquest while there went
Those years and years by of world without event
That in Majorca Alfonso watched the door.

Centred in my own self-reliance and hyperactivity, I have often recognized in others such total commitment to social concern that they have had no time, no space for God in prayer. From such foundations, however good the intention, there is a spiritual dimension missing which impoverishes their lives and work.

This book explores the growth and development in the spiritual life, outlook and teaching of four mystics. Three are male members of different religious orders and one a lay woman; two are medieval, two modern. This may seem a strange grouping but Terry Tastard's purpose is very important for the world of today. Though they are very individual and each gives a unique insight, they have much in common in their contemplation and the gradual evolution which breaks through the polarization I have been talking about earlier. Because of this contemplation linking to and developing into concern for the desperate needs of today's world there is a good hope that there may be a wider acceptance of a spirituality which is effective in the midst of the escalating injustice and lack of peace all over the world at the present time.

It is a constant wonder that the Lord touches each individual so individually. It is also important to realize that God's work often, perhaps normally, takes a long time. Not enough weight is given to this education which God works in and with each person. Because of this, men and women dash off in different directions or take up extreme positions, only modifying their outlook after years, and becoming much more effective through the distillation of prayer, meditation and concern for the pain of the world.

Christ draws all to himself when he is lifted up. But with the gaze centred on Jesus Christ and him crucified, it is easily possible to forget what went before his public life, his suffering and his death on the cross. In fact, Jesus spent some thirty years 'hidden'. It was during this time that he was learning to be man, for God had never been man before Christ. He was learning the world from a human perspective, learning to work out his Father's will in the human situation, until the right time came and the Spirit fired him to preach the good news to the poor.

Sometimes the awfulness of the world, the absence of love, of peace and of justice drives people to despise and thrust aside the slower growth in wider and deeper awareness. But, as is evident in the stories of the four mystics at the centre of this book, time, thought, prayer, space and regular commitment emerge into a remarkable depth of understanding of God, from which also emerges a spark of fire which unites the knowledge and love of God with the knowledge and love of the world. This in turn opens a fire of energy in the pursuit of justice, peace and love in the world.

To absorb the message of these pages requires more than a swift and superficial reading. It is necessary to ponder what is written so that the thoughts may kindle in the reader the fusion of love of God and desire for helping to create a world society of justice, peace and love, which is not left to somebody else, or a mere wordy discussion, but is the implanted seed in you which will emerge to be a fire of love for justice and peace such as Christ declared when he said that he had come to cast fire on the earth and he wanted it to be kindled.

MICHAEL HOLLINGS

Acknowledgements

During the writing of this book I have realized more than ever how important my friends are to me. To them, and to my brothers and sisters in community, I would like to give my thanks for their supportive love. Community also put up with the whirr and clack of the word processor and with the brewing of endless cups of tea. I am particularly grateful for the inspiration and friendship given to me over the years by Michael Hollings, Grace Jantzen and John Townroe.

I would also like to thank the Catholic Central Library and Dr Williams' Library, both in London, for valuable assistance given.

TERRY TASTARD SSF

1

Finding Another Way

Contemporary developments in our late-twentieth-century world repeatedly pose a challenge to all aspects of Christian faith, including spirituality. The challenge is to show the significance of our faith in the struggle for a better world. Our crisis is a global one: we have so many problems together that we can only find the answers together. Countries as far apart as Peru and Tanzania struggle to repay debts owed to northern hemisphere bankers. Emissions from power stations in Britain fall as acid rain in Scandinavia. French nuclear testing in the Pacific produces fall-out in Australia. Even within countries the links become obvious: in Britain, for example, hospitals struggle with underfunding while taxation is cut. Problems such as these have created new expectations of the Christian conscience, both inside and outside the church.

A British theologian visiting a poor quarter in San Jose, Costa Rica recorded the following conversation. A woman had started a neighbourhood group to work for improvements in the area; her friend protested that this was the job of local government officials. The woman replied by asking:

'Do you believe in Jesus Christ?'
'Yes.'
'Do you think Jesus Christ came to change life so that it was more the kind of life God wanted to see, or to leave it as it is?'
'I suppose to change it. Yes, to change it.'

1

'Do you think Jesus Christ means to change life by him-self, or did he mean us to share the work with him?'

(Hesitantly) 'I know he meant us to play a part.'

'Then how can you believe in Jesus Christ and let things stay as they are?'[1]

How can you believe in Jesus Christ and let things stay as they are? This is the question Christians ask themselves. It is even sometimes found on the lips of people of other faiths (or no faith). And so it is natural that we ask how that aspect of our faith which we call spirituality helps us; how does it enable us to join others in working today for a better tomorrow to be shared by all people?

Whatever the answer is, it has to be one which does not drive us into the swamps of guilt. Christians are often made to care about contemporary issues through a dangerous mixture of guilt and encouragement. Encouragement is shouted at us to be vigilant about this ominous trend or that oppressive country, to give to this charity or go to that meeting, to join this demonstration or that boycott. Yet the energy we have is inevitably limited. Discovering where and how we can best make our contribution to social justice is not easy. I firmly believe that Christians should be active in social concern, and later I will give some examples of how this can be done. But I believe that tackled the wrong way – and especially tackled through guilt – exhaustion and disillusionment can set in. Certainly to be a Christian today requires us to be committed to social change. But this commitment needs to come from deep within us. We need to build up an inner disposition which will enable us to act freely in the struggle for justice and peace, and which will give us both discernment and staying-power.

In this respect free action from within is always better than obedience to instructions from without. The tiny spark in the car's engine gives it more power and greater efficiency than ten people pushing it. Analogously we need a social involve-ment that flows from a strong personal spirituality rather than a social involvement that springs from a mixture of guilt

2

and exhortation. In other words we will go further and achieve more if we have a prayerful, loving knowledge of God to motivate our social concern.

It is worth noting in passing that not every spirituality helps us assume our social responsibilities. For example, when the Dominican writer Antony Archer looked back at Roman Catholic life in Britain's cities before the Second Vatican Council he was struck by how liturgy and doctrine combined to make the church a refuge from life. This spirituality was symbolized by the timeless, frozen nature of the Tridentine mass, presented as if it were unrelated to any particular culture or situation. He concludes that at that time:

> the Christian hope for the future was focused on individual and personal salvation without wider reference. For these sorts of reasons, when changes began to take place in the neighbourhood the church was not as such able to respond. The priests could only continue with their visiting, crossing off their lists the streets that were being bulldozed by the Council and noting that these and those families were no longer living in the area. There was no way that they or anyone else could envisage the church, exclusively concerned as it was with the sacred, doing anything else.[2]

It is summed up by the comment made by a Catholic layperson looking back at that period: 'Religion wasn't carried into one's life. Religion consisted of going *into* church.'[3] I have cited a Catholic example, but examples could be given of other churches creating spiritualities which led to a detachment from society and its problems. Looking critically at the past in this way is not necessarily discouraging. Indeed it can encourage by showing us how far we have come, for today the test of a spirituality is its ability to help us deepen both our love of God and our commitment to change the face of the earth.

Faced with the urgency and scale of our contemporary social problems, the temptation is to seek a spirituality which places the primary emphasis on social service. Yet this proves,

I believe, less satisfactory than a spirituality which helps us discover the love of God, and God's love for the world. When a person is drawn into the divine love, a liberation can take place which enables that person to be a force for social change. This can happen through new energies being given, or a greater insight into the needs of the world. Sometimes the person develops a critical faculty which penetrates society's self-deceptions and enables him or her to resist injustice.

Yet love of God is not known in a vacuum. Jürgen Moltmann says that theology today has to be present to its times, to its situation, not just in a chronological sense but in a kairological sense. He is drawing here on the difference between the two Greek words for time in the New Testament: *chronos*, which means time in the sense of the passage of time, and *kairos*, time in the sense of the right moment, the challenge of a particular situation emerging at a given time. When theologians in South Africa met to draw up a theological comment on the political crisis there, they called it *The Kairos Document*. They explained: 'Kairos is the Greek word that is used in the Bible to designate a special moment of time when God visits his people to offer them a unique opportunity for repentance and conversion, for change and decisive action. It is a moment of truth, a crisis.'[4] Thus, for example, we read in the gospel according to Luke that Jesus weeps over Jerusalem because it had chosen to ignore the things that made for peace. Jesus speaks as if to the whole city, saying that as a result of its blindness destruction will come its way, 'all because you did not recognize your opportunity (*kairon*) when God offered it' (Lk. 19:44). *Kairos* is the time to act decisively that breaks with past patterns. And we recognize these potential turning-points to the extent that we are attuned to the realities in the world around us.

When Moltmann looks at what it means for theology to be kairologically present, he comments that this asks much more than just adaptation to changing circumstances:

Making theology present cannot just be a matter of adaptation to the spirit of modern times; it must also be participation in the sufferings of this time and resistance to those who cause them. The saving and liberating potential of the historical recollection of Christ . . . first becomes evident through participation in the history of suffering in the present, by taking the side of the victims of the 'modern world'.[5]

What is true of theology must also be true of spirituality. A spirituality for our times needs to be kairologically present. That is, a genuine spirituality will be one which helps us deepen our awareness of the suffering of the world around us, and empowers us to do something about it. And it is impossible to enter into the reality of such situations without being caught up in some way in the suffering. As Moltmann reminds us, sharing in suffering is part of what it means to be kairologically present.

This combination of the love of God and being present to our times is what I mean by 'the spark in the soul', a metaphor I take from Eckhart. Where our heart warms responsively to God's love of us, and at the same time we enter more deeply into the reality of life on our planet, there we have a personal spirituality which can enable our involvement in social action. The spark in the soul comes when we hold fast to both God and the world. Love of God who made and loves the world enables us to grow in love of the world. Entry into fuller knowledge of the world, particularly through standing alongside those who suffer in it, enables us to know and do God's will. The spark in the soul is our heart responding in love to God and the world. The more we do this, the more it increases our ability to do both. After all there is no limit to our potential growth in love, and we advance in love by doing it.

In speaking of the spark in the soul I am therefore trying to combine our personal experience of the love of God and our consciousness of the suffering and difficulties of our world. Both radicals and conservatives tend to be suspicious of such an approach. The radical voice says that to work is to pray, and to help one's fellows *is* to love God. Traditional methods of spiritual growth, such as silence, solitude, prayer of adoration, are looked on as flight from engagement with the world. The conservative voice says that only individuals can be converted, and that to change society we have to convert as many people as possible. Joining with others in social action is seen as an evasion of the challenge to personal discipleship. In giving this account I am painting, of course, with a broad brush, and no doubt many exceptions could be found. For example, the late Dorothy Day was a traditional Roman Catholic with a love of daily mass, the rosary and prayer in front of the Blessed Sacrament. Her strong personal spirituality, however, strengthened her prophetic witness in establishing houses of hospitality for the poor and supporting strikers and war-resisters. Another counter-example, this time from the Evangelical tradition, would be Jim Wallis, leader of the Sojourners Community in Washington, with whom he shares a ministry to the poor and bold prophetic witness.

Despite such exceptions I think it is true to say that the division in the church today between radical and conservative is now more basic than the former division between Catholic and Evangelical traditions. Catholic and Evangelical Christians can be found on both sides of the radical/conservative divide. This affects spirituality as much as any other aspect of church life. Yet I do not believe that the radical/conservative polarization is necessary in spirituality, and I will be drawing on four mystics to show how a personal spirituality can enable and sustain social change. I believe that it is appropriate to turn to these four mystics because they showed precisely the combination of love of God and commitment to social justice which I believe is necessary for our times. I am not arguing that these four lived out an identical spirituality – indeed our study will bring out some differences. But it is true that all of them seem to have had an intense experience of the love of God as the underlying reality of the world. Perhaps because of this, they were able to hold together, in different ways, their relationship with God and their links with the world, in a way that empowered them to act for change in the world. Surprisingly often the truth about the mystics contradicts their popular image. Mystics tend to be thought of as people who fled the world; they often turn out to be people creatively engaged with it. Where there is flight it is often flight from the shallowness, delusions or sickness of the world.

I have chosen two medieval mystics, Francis of Assisi and Meister Eckhart; and two modern ones, Evelyn Underhill and Thomas Merton. From Francis' discovery of the vulnerability of God we learn about seeing through the eyes of the poor. This leads on to how Francis' meditation on Christ's presence in our sufferings deepened his awareness of the suffering people of his day. We also discover in Francis a spirituality of non-violence.

Meister Eckhart teaches us how detachment from the world's distractions helps us recover our consciousness of God within us as the ground of our being. This contradicts contemporary teaching on human nature, which tells us that we are more human the more we possess as consumers. Eckhart also leads us to a sense of ourselves as the place of God's birth-giving, where the world is made anew through God's transforming presence in us.

Evelyn Underhill shows how complete prayer includes adoration, communion and co-operation. Love of God challenges us to get involved in completing his purposes through our free co-operation; co-operation in turn challenges us to see through any distortions and false perceptions of society. Prayer implies our acceptance of change.

Thomas Merton points us towards a discovery of our identity in God and not in terms of role or achievement. He encourages us to enter into solitude and silence, which will help break down the prejudices which we inherit from society; it will help us see officially promoted lies for what they are and reach beyond them for the truth. Finally his teaching on contemplation draws our attention to a contemporary sickness, which views the world and other people as important only in so far as they are useful.

I ought to say at this point that I read Eckhart from a Franciscan perspective. I belong to a Franciscan religious order, and it has always been the Franciscan tradition to emphasize the power of love, whereas the Dominican tradition emphasizes the power of the awakened mind. Eckhart was a Dominican. My reading of him may give a greater role to the power of love in his spirituality than is usually the case. In this sense I am offering a personal interpretation of Eckhart. But I believe it to be a fair one, in that it draws attention to what his spirituality offers those who approach it in that way. I ought also to say that by 'spark in the soul' he means a particular aspect of human nature. I use the metaphor rather differently, and to avoid confusion I do not use it in Chapter 3 where I look at Eckhart. Of the four mystics examined he is the one of whom we have the least biographical information. The quantity of his writings and the richness of their content, however, allow us to make some important inferences about his thinking with regard to society in his day. Finally with regard to Eckhart, the reader should remember that he is a creative philosopher and theologian. Although I have simplified what he has to say, there are inevitably some abstract and difficult parts to this chapter. The reader who finds it hard going could go on to subsequent chapters and return to Eckhart later.

With all four mystics I believe that we can learn both from what they taught and from how they lived their lives. This is because they were present to their times in the sense of knowing the *kairos*, the time of choosing, which was confronting them. As Moltman reminds us, if we and our spirituality would be present to our times, then we must be able to enter into and in some way share the sufferings of the world's victims, of those people who are used and held to be of little account. And we need to be present in a way that strengthens us to act in accordance with the challenge of the *kairos*, the choices that have to be made. German theologian Walbert Buhlmann says that a new spirituality is being born in today's world, a spirituality 'where there is less talk about humility, obedience and piety and more about courage, risk and involvement in transforming the world'.[6] The four mystics we are about to look at help us understand what this new spirituality can be like, and help us enter into it. If Christians succeed in making a strong contribution to justice and peace, it will be because they have been able to embrace both God and the world, the dual movement which I am calling the spark in the soul. And where this exists, the capacity for such love is steadily deepened.

A spirituality of commitment to action can sound a daunting thing. It can seem to imply a great cost to the person concerned. There can be a great cost, and there can even be a kind of burnout as people go beyond their personal resources. But that is not the whole picture. My own involvement with justice and peace groups has been greatly encouraging. The people I have found in them have often been people of great hope, of good humour, of sincerity and honesty, openness and trust. They have also shown all the usual human frailties. But there has been a happiness among them precisely because they have been doing what they could in response to God's love of the world. Sometimes people – even ourselves – think that happiness lies in evading that challenge. The temptation is to believe that happiness can be found by giving the priority to self-interest defined in a narrow way. But does this lead to happiness? Consider what the Brazilian theologian Clodovis Boff had to say about his perceptions of Europe:

The pessimism and scepticism of Europeans can, literally, be seen on the faces. As a friend said to me after returning from a period of time in old Europe. 'Europeans look like people who have eaten something which disagreed with them.' It's true. Europeans may have more than enough, but remain (perhaps for that reason) resentful, suspicious and disillusioned. They lack just what our people have in abundance, despite being broken, toothless, illiterate, thin and ill-clad, namely hope. Their hope can be seen in the brightness of faces, the spark of eyes, the energy of language and human relations, in an enjoyment of life, in spite of everything.[7]

This is a generalization, of course. But it is an honest

testimony from a visitor from Latin America, and other visitors from other southern hemisphere countries have made similar comments over the years. Why this difference? I suggest that it is because the faith of people in the two-thirds world convinces them that the future is open. They can work to make a change. Their present sacrifice can bear fruit in a better tomorrow. With this spark in their soul people in a country like Brazil can find freedom even in the midst of injustice and want. They stand assured that God is with them and that he encourages them to take responsibility for their own lives. My hope is that in the northern hemisphere we can find a similar spirituality which gives us life and hope and frees us to commit ourselves.

1   Ian M. Fraser, *The Fire Runs* (London, 1975), p. 9.
2   Antony Archer, *The Two Catholic Churches: a study in oppression* (London, 1986), pp. 102–3.
3   ibid., p. 99.
4   *The Kairos Document*, CIIR, Third World Theology ser., 2nd rev. edn (London, 1986), p. 33. They cite as scriptural examples Mk 1:15; Lk 8:13; 19:44; Rom. 13:11–13; 1 Cor. 7:29; 2 Cor. 6:2; Tit. 1:3; Rev. 1:3; 22:10.
5   Jürgen Moltmann, *Theology Today* (London, 1988), p. ix.
6   Walbert Buhlmann, 'Toward a theology of peace' in *Theology Digest*, vol. 31, no. 2 (1984), p. 138.
7   Clodovis Boff, *The Way Forward for the First World Church*, CIIR, Third World Theology ser. (London, 1986), p. 6.

2

St Francis of Assisi and God in Our Midst

Rarely can any person have been as much betrayed by his popular image as Francis of Assisi. Francis was a strong person who was acutely conscious of the desperate poverty and suffering around him. In his commitment to peace-making and to justice for the poor he was prepared to defy public opinion and the conventions of his time. Yet the popular image is of a happy-go-lucky inoffensive saint who loved animals and preached to birds. People tend to focus on Francis with an interest in the picturesque, and the result, in the words of a French Franciscan scholar, is 'a pretty story of the birds and the wolf or the rabbit, with the hero becoming creation's superficial prince'.[1] The time has come for us to recover a fuller picture of Francis of Assisi, particularly since he has much to teach us on how we can deepen our prayer life in a way that will help us work for justice and peace.

We can learn many lessons from Francis. Central to Francis' life and teaching was his awe at God's choice of vulnerability, a choice made by God out of the depth of God's love for us. We learn from Francis the importance of the image of God to whom we pray and out of whose love we act. Francis teaches us to look for God among the powerless and the poor. A second lesson from Francis is that he teaches us the importance of compassion. This means growing in our ability to see through the eyes of others. Thirdly Francis shows us how to live a spirituality of non-violence. Each of these lessons can set us at odds with society's received wisdom. I will develop the three lessons later in the chapter,

11

but first I want to explain why in many ways Francis' times resemble ours.

Francis in his times

Francis of Assisi was born in 1181 or 1182 and died in 1226. It might be thought that the medieval period could scarcely be more different from our own. Yet on closer examination we find that Francis lived in times that shared many of the pressures and problems of the late twentieth century. It is partly because Francis was shaped by the society around him and spoke to its concerns that he is able to speak to us so trenchantly today.

He lived in an era of accelerated social change. Historians estimate that between 1050 and 1300 the population of Europe trebled, with particularly rapid growth of towns and cities.[2] It was moreover a time of economic revolution. Europe's economy shifted from being one of gift and barter to being one of profit and investment. There was a vast expansion of coinage through new mintings, and banking began to develop, particularly through the use of letters of credit. Francis' lifespan corresponds almost exactly with the formation of the first commercial companies, and there was a great expansion of trade.[3] These rapid developments brought new pressures to bear on western European society.

In every age there are popular stories or tales, sometimes with a humorous twist, that are told to illustrate some kind of moral. Over time we can observe that the human weaknesses attacked by the tales change, as society itself changes. So we can observe, for example, that in the period around Francis avarice begins to replace pride as the most prominent vice figuring in such legends.[4] (Are we in the middle of another such change? Is avarice once more reappearing, this time to replace lust as the 'deadly sin' of which we are most conscious?) From these legends and other Middle Ages sources we know that there was considerable disgust with the wickedness of city life and unease at the obsession with money-

making. Many people seem to have felt that society's institutions were being corrupted. The situation was made more
unstable by the juxtaposition of extremes of wealth and poverty created by commercial development and the population
explosion. Historian Rosalind Brooke notes that in the earlier
Middle Ages destitution was comparatively rare except in
times of war or famine. Poverty was generally seen as a
product of factors such as old age or illness, and no stigma
attached to it, because:

> its sufferers were individually known and were normally
> supported by the solidarity of the family, the village, the
> parish, the abbey. . . But with the increase of population,
> urbanisation, mobility, trade, the disintegration of the
> traditional order and relationships, deficiencies of pro-
> duction and distribution, rising prices, wealth and oppor-
> tunities grew, and also the numbers of the poor. More
> and more flocked to the towns, where [they] . . . lived in
> collective, anonymous misery and want.[5]

Some of these pressures were reflected in attitudes towards
the church, which was criticized for its growing wealth and
increasing remoteness from ordinary people. There was a
desire for the church to make what we would today call an
option for the poor. Some of this desire was expressed in
initiatives by lay people who formed groups such as the Humi-
liati and the Waldensians, which emphasized a simple lifestyle, personal fidelity to Jesus' teachings and looking after
the needs of the poor. Sometimes this desire took an explosive
form, such as the movement led by Arnold of Brescia, a priest
who was executed in 1155 but remained very much part of
Italian folklore in Francis' time. Arnold preached against the
wealth and corruption of the church and led the people of
Rome into revolt. The papacy only succeeded in re-establish-
ing itself there and crushing Arnold with the help of the
emperor.

This then is the world into which Francis of Assisi
was born and in which he grew up, a world with many

resemblances to our own: a world of accelerated social change, of unease at the extremes of wealth and poverty, a world in which economically, socially and religiously the old order was painfully changing into the new.

Turning-points in Francis' life

Francis himself felt the influence of these changes. His father Pietro Bernardone was a prosperous cloth merchant who benefited from Europe's fast-changing economy, with its better banking and booming trade fairs. As a cloth merchant Pietro Bernardone also profited from the sophisticated tastes of the wealthy as they sought to be dressed fashionably. Francis' parents strove to give their much-loved son the best things in life. Not surprisingly he turned out to be spoilt, but with an insouciant charm that dissolved the exasperation of his parents. Something of a playboy, he had many friends and a popularity helped, one suspects, by the liberality with which his indulgent father gave him money. His early biographer, Thomas of Celano, who knew Francis personally writes that Francis in his carefree youth:

> strove to outdo the rest in the pomp of vainglory, in jokes, in strange doings, in idle and useless talk, in songs, in soft and flowing garments, for he was very rich . . . a squanderer of all his possessions. . . On the other hand he was a very kindly person, easy and affable, even making himself foolish because of it; for because of these qualities many ran after him. . .[6]

After this description we might think of Francis as being something of a fool, but in fact Thomas of Celano also records that he had a sharp business sense. So we conclude that Francis was a party-loving, rather self-indulgent young man who enjoyed company, a snappy dresser who wanted to be admired by his peers.

When and how did his conversion take place? Put that way

the question will produce a misleading answer. Francis had a number of important turning-points in his life. To choose one or two as the moment of conversion is a mistake, because Francis sought to live conversion. Despite all that he had achieved, near the end of his life he said to his followers, in all sincerity, 'Let us begin, brothers, to serve the Lord God, for up to now we have made little or no progress.'[7] So although I will mention some major turning-points in Francis' life, we should see them as arising out of his ongoing pilgrimage.

Around the end of 1204 Francis had barely set off for a military campaign in Apulia when he turned back in response to a dream message which left him unhappy about weapons of war. Not long afterwards he began the process of living in poverty, first by selling his goods then by giving away his money, a process which brought him into conflict with his family and led Francis to strip himself naked before the Bishop of Assisi as a sign that he owed his family nothing and was beginning a new life. He now began to look after the poor and the sick and to live a life of prayer in poverty. He was fortified in this process by an experience of prayer in front of a crucifix in San Damiano, on the outskirts of Assisi, when Christ instructed him to repair his ruined church. In February 1208 Francis heard Matthew 10:6–10 read at mass, in which Jesus instructs his followers to go and preach the kingdom. Francis immediately felt that this was God's will for him. He became a preacher, and gave away what few extra clothes he had; the gospel, after all, commanded him to do this and to go barefoot as well. Within a year eleven others had joined him, and his fledgling order had, against all the odds, won papal approval for its rule.

Francis began an itinerant lifestyle: preaching repentance and visiting the communities of his mushrooming order to exhort and encourage them (within a few years there were 5000 brothers). He travelled as far afield as Dalmatia, Spain, Egypt and the Holy Land. Direction of the order began increasingly to slip out of his hands, and in 1220 he resigned its leadership. Hitherto Francis' conversion process had been one of action and commitment. Now, increasingly, his conversion went forward in prayer and suffering. During the course of a long retreat in solitude on Mount La Verna in 1224 the marks of the stigmata – the wounds of the crucified Christ – appeared on him and were to stay with him for the rest of his life, bleeding intermittently. Other suffering came his way, notably the loss of his eyesight. Yet during this last period of his life Francis drew closer to God. Francis was able to write lyrical praises of God in the Canticle of the Creatures during this time, and also to reconcile bishop and mayor in a divided Assisi. He died on 3 October 1226, laid naked on the ground at his own request in a last gesture of faithfulness to the poverty he had freely undertaken years previously.

So what were the turning-points in Francis' life? The answer to this question provides the key to understanding how Francis helps us develop a spirituality for social change. It is easy, but misleading, to see Francis led forward by a few 'supernatural' events: the experience in front of the crucifix at San Damiano, the sense of vocation on hearing Matthew 10 read, the stigmata on La Verna. But this is only part of the picture. The fuller picture is that Francis' experiences of society fed into his life of prayer, which in turn led him back into society. In this sense Francis' spirituality was dialectical, moving between, and integrating, the two poles of involvement in God and involvement in society, the one leading to the other and back again. In the metaphor I am using, Francis' spirituality was that of the spark in the soul, holding together love of God and love of the world. As part of this process he became acutely aware of the suffering of people around him, and shared their suffering. In this way his spirituality was present to his times. Francis himself draws our attention to this process, in which God drew him to the poor who then deepened his conversion. In his Testament, written near the end of his life, Francis begins by saying that God inspired him by leading him to live among lepers: 'When I had once become acquainted with them, what had previously nauseated me became a source of spiritual and physical consolation for me. After that I did not wait long before leaving the world.'[8] The importance of these words is underscored by their being for us the opening words of the dictation of a dying man, his ultimate message. He tells us that his experience of life among the most wretched of society was a fundamental influence in his whole commitment to God.

This point needs further developing, and I shall attempt to do this by considering what Francis has to teach us regarding our image of God. I will then go on to look at what we can learn from him regarding compassion and non-violence. I believe that from these aspects of Francis' life and teaching we can learn how to pray in a way that will also lead us deeper into social involvement.

The vulnerable God

The aspect of God that above all seized Francis' heart was God's willingness to set aside his glory. Francis' spirituality was thus highly kenotic, that is, one which treasured the memory of God's self-emptying love. This spirituality focused on God's self-revelation in poverty and human vulnerability. From the first day when faith in God came alive for him, Francis was deeply moved by the knowledge that God had humbled himself out of love for us. This was fundamental to Francis' whole outlook: that the infinite God had chosen, in Jesus, to express himself through the confines of human flesh. The same God, God of everlastingness beyond time, had chosen to enter history not only in Jesus of Nazareth but in the ongoing eucharistic presence of Jesus. Francis never lost an opportunity to drive home the humility shown by God in his overwhelming love for us, speaking with amazement at how, daily in the Eucharist, 'In his love, God gives himself into our hands.'[9] A God who sets aside his power so that we with our poor, limited capacities for understanding can see and grasp and sense him – this was the God that Francis sought to bring home to any who would hear him. 'He was rich beyond measure, and yet he . . . chose poverty,' writes Francis in a letter addressed to all Christians.[10] Francis saw quite clearly the paradox that God's greatness is expressed

17

in poverty and vulnerability, and he wanted this to be a source of life for those who followed him as Franciscans. Thus in the Rule of 1223 we find Francis writing that brothers should not be ashamed of poverty, 'because God made himself poor for us in this world'.[11] In his biography of Francis, Bonaventure notes that 'The memory of the poverty felt by Christ and his Mother often reduced him to tears'; Bonaventure adds that Francis often quoted Jesus' words from Matthew 8:20, that foxes had holes and birds their nests, but the Son of Man nowhere to lay his head.[12] The image of God that moved Francis, then, was the memory of God who had made himself known in poverty and its accompanying vulnerability. This was for Francis the supreme proof of God's love for us, and Francis responded to it with all the love that he could muster. His response of love was part of the spark in Francis' soul which led him to want to follow God's own path of risk-taking in love and setting-aside of self. He was able to be open to the world's pain because he was following a God who had similarly entered into the reality of human vulnerability and suffering.

Francis wanted to imitate God out of love for God's love. This spirituality of Francis' was not one of passivity. It was one that was rich in action for and with the poor, and for this reason I believe that it offers valuable lessons today if we are seeking to pray in a way that increases our commitment to social change. I suggested earlier that in Francis we see a rhythm in which prayer and experience feed into one another in a process of mutual deepening. This dynamic process is the heart of spirituality, and we see it clearly at work in Francis' openness to the poor, to lepers, and even to robbers. In 1204 or 1205 Francis turned back from the journey to warfare in Apulia, and after giving away his wealth and parting from his family, went to live with lepers. We are told that he washed them and cleaned their wounds[13] and 'served them with loving eagerness'.[14] He began to help other poor people too, 'stretching forth a hand of mercy to those who had nothing, and showing compassion to the afflicted'.[15]

What sort of process was at work in Francis here? As we

saw earlier, in his Testament Francis gives us important insight into a conversion process that was to permeate his whole life:

> This is how God inspired me Brother Francis, to embark upon a life of penance. When I was in sin, the sight of lepers nauseated me beyond measure; but then God himself led me into their company, and I had pity on them. When I had once become acquainted with them, what had previously nauseated me became a source of spiritual and physical consolation for me.[16]

Note that for Francis this was an experience of God. This in itself was remarkable. Medieval society was strongly hierarchical. The image of God that was conveyed nearly everywhere was of God as a triumphant judge, an awe-inspiring monarch who was at the top of a many-tiered universe. Actually the predominant image of God in western Europe was already beginning to change before Francis came on the scene. Much of this movement was the work of Cistercian writers such as Bernard of Clairvaux (1090–1153), who brought a new affective spirituality. He wrote of Christ as the Beloved lover of the Songs of Songs, and developed a devotion to the wounds of Jesus. He was also one of many medieval writers – including Anselm of Canterbury and Aelred of Rievaulx – who used motherly images such as breasts and nurturing to describe Christ. This human, loving, suffering Christ was a big change from the previously emphasized timeless Christ, all-powerful judge of the universe. Franciscans, following the emphases of Francis himself, played a key role in popularizing this developing understanding of God's love in Christ. The change owed much to the strong Franciscan presence in towns, and to their ability to preach and write in a homely, accessible way.

This development in spirituality reflected Francis' own experience. Francis found God through the poor; lepers mediated the divine presence for him. Francis had already been seeking God in silence, in solitude and in poverty, but henceforth he was to have a clearer understanding and deeper love of the God who sets aside his power out of humble love for us. In today's language we might say that Francis was evangelized by the poor, as he himself makes clear by saying how much *they* gave *him*.

At the same time Francis was empowered by a changed understanding of God. After living among the poor, Francis was to be drawn more and more to God's face revealed in the poverty and suffering of Christ. The influence of this experience emerges in the Rule of 1221 in which Francis writes: 'The friars should be delighted to follow the lowliness and poverty of our Lord Jesus Christ. . . They should be glad to live among social outcasts, among the poor and helpless, the sick and the lepers, and those who beg by the wayside.'[17] And Francis also makes it clear that 'Everyone who comes to them, friend or foe, rogue or robber, must be made welcome.'[18] Francis' image of God, and his integration of experience into prayer, brought him to this point. And we diminish it greatly if we see it simply in terms of Francis doing good works. After all, by first living among and then welcoming with open arms the poor, the lepers and the robbers, Francis was throwing a challenge at society. Groups are always partly defined by whom they exclude. Francis, by contrast, wants to create a different, inclusive understanding of community in which the formerly outcast are drawn into its heart. This spirituality inverts society's categories: writing about the first Franciscan brothers, Thomas of Celano says that they stayed 'in the houses of lepers, or *in other decent places*'.[19] From the poverty and vulnerability of life shared with the poor the first Franciscans were brought to a position where they did not share society's categories. Their spirituality had been a subversive experience. Their spirituality of the spark in the soul had combined love of God and love of the poor in a way that turned society's conventions of decency upside-down.

Spirituality carries connotations of peace to many people, of resting securely in the love of God and knowing happiness in that love. This is certainly an important aspect of spirituality. But the experiences of Francis and his first followers remind us that our spirituality can also be a disturbing factor in our lives, one that shakes our preconceptions and leads us to question society's conventional wisdom. Franciscan spirituality focuses on God's self-emptying love and entry into human vulnerability. I would suggest that anyone seeking to live Franciscan spirituality in Britain or the United States today ought to feel in some way apart from national trends. Recent years in these countries has seen a cult of power. Strong leadership has been emphasized, and the interests of the poorest and weakest members of society have been discounted in favour of submission to a particular concept of economic efficiency. Accumulation (of power, money, opportunity) has been the controlling image in national life. Giving away has not been favoured, except when it is seen as charity and thus always leaves the giver in control.

With Francis in mind, we need to ask what image of God we and others around us have at the heart of our spirituality. Every society has a tendency to make God in its own image. In Chapter 5 I mention Thomas Merton's criticisms of the United States in this respect. In Britain too, however, there is a problematic image of God. We tend to think of God rather as we think of the monarch at the head of the nation (or, significantly, at the head of the Church of England). The monarch reigns impartially, above the ebb and flow of political crisis and social need, concerned but not involved. The monarch certainly can have no personal views on whether our social system is skewed in favour of the rich and powerful and to keep the poor and powerless in their place. There is an implicit tendency in Britain – or, more correctly, in England – to view God in the same way, as neither taking sides nor suffering with his people. Francis, however, points us in a different direction. He reminds us that God is already present in the poor: in the homeless on the streets and in cheap hotels, among the unemployed and those made 'redundant', among the elderly who live in loneliness and the people who feel trapped in pockets of urban decay. God is there because it is God's nature and God's choice to make himself known in vulnerability. And God's choice of vulnerability is never

21

intended to allow things to stay as they are. Rather it is a demonstration of his love that reaches out within human need and seeks a transformation of all that crushes and oppresses. This too was seen by Francis. In a passage that captures the flavour of Francis' own God-imitating love, Bonaventure writes: 'Francis . . . immediately referred to Christ the poverty or deprivation he saw in anyone. . . His soul melted at the sight of the poor or infirm and where he could not offer material assistance he lavished his affection. . . Francis saw Christ's image in every poor person he met.'[20] Likewise Thomas of Celano in a similar passage says that whenever Francis saw a person in poverty he envisaged it as happening to Christ: 'Thus in all the poor he saw the Son of the poor lady, and he bore naked in his heart whom she bore naked in her hands.'[21]

From Francis then, we learn two interlinked lessons. First he reminds us that God came to us through self-emptying love in which he became vulnerable in Christ. Second Francis shows us how an encounter with the poor can be an encounter with God speaking to us through their need. Francis is thus challenging us to find the spark in our own soul, which flares up when our love responds to the risk-taking love of God.

How do we respond to the love of God with a love which similarly disposes us to take risks? The temptation at this point is always to begin to debate whether or not it is possible to imitate the poverty of Francis or, in our own day, Mother Teresa of Calcutta. Yet I think that this is often to miss the point about what Francis was doing. By living with the poor and making a place for them in society, Francis was making a profoundly prophetic gesture. (I return to this point when talking about compassion.) Francis was resisting the society of his day which would have swept the lepers out of sight and pretended that the poor were not really needy. It is a point noted by Leonardo Boff, who says that Francis' action in going to the margin of society was 'a protest and an act of love – a *protest* against a society that expels the poor from its midst and hides them in inhuman places outside the mainstream of life'.[22] This is, in biblical terms, truly prophetic work, for the prophetic task is to break through what Old Testament scholar Walter Brueggemann calls the 'dominant consciousness'.[23] Brueggemann draws our attention to how in the time of Solomon, for instance, we find a society in which the dominant consciousness justified affluence for the few, and as part of this stressed social order at the expense of justice. The prophetic task was to articulate the pain of those whose suffering paid for the prosperity and well-being of the dominant class. In such a situation, 'Bringing hurt to public expression is an important first step in the dismantling criticism that permits a new reality.'[24] This was the critical thrust of Francis' action in making his home with the poor and rejected. A few people may have that literal option today: living with the mentally handicapped in Jean Vanier's l'Arche communities, for instance, or joining Simon communities to live with the homeless. All of us, however, have the option of following Francis (and the Old Testament prophets) in seeking to make the poor and the suffering heard and visible. There is, then, a close link between the spark in our soul and the political and social policies that we support.

We will have no choice but to become committed to work for change in society, because we will be seeing society through the eyes of the poor. The Argentinian theologian Jose Miguez Bonino says that there are two ways of viewing society. One approach is the 'functional' one, which views society from the top, from the point of view of those who wield power or enjoy security. From this angle society seems a basically satisfactory system in need of preservation and perfecting. The alternative is what Bonino calls the 'dialectical' approach, seeing society from the point of view of the poor and the voiceless. From this angle society will seem 'inadequate, badly structured, full of conflict and in need of transformation'.[25] If we follow Francis then there is no choice but to adopt the latter approach. We may even find that it enables us to share a little of his vulnerability. People who bring the message of society's hidden suffering are neither welcome nor respected. It will do us no good at all to be speaking up or demonstrating for the homeless of our bed and breakfast hotels and our city streets. It does not make us popular to resist pride in our armed forces bought at the price of shame in our hospitals. In this respect our spirituality will have important implications for social change. This, of course, raises the question of how we can more strongly link our prayer life with involvement in society. Francis points us to compassion in answer to this question.

Compassion

The topic of compassion is frequently found on the lips of politicians, but do they use it correctly? Or do they misconceive the true nature of compassion? Politicians today commend compassion because they want to be seen as generous to the poor. We are told that in so far as British people are successful economically, they can and should reach out to the poorest and neediest to help them with the profits of success. In essence we are being told that the poor need more charity. But is this compassion?

The etymology of the word is interesting. It comes from the Latin words *com + passio*, meaning to suffer with. Compassion is strongly linked with empathy. It means to suffer with, in the sense of to feel with a person in distress, and it implies a strong fellow-feeling. It is to be moved to do something about the cause of the other person's pain, which has in a sense become one's own. Although the Latin origin of compassion shares another root, this time a Greek one, with the English word sympathy, their meaning has drifted apart in contemporary English. With its connotation of standing alongside, of sharing feeling, compassion is different from sympathy. Sympathy will tend to result in charity. It can leave the giver comparatively unmoved, and is addressed to the immediate occasion of need rather than the cause. When politicians speak of compassion they generally mean sympathy.

Francis was someone who was acutely aware of other people's feelings when they were suffering. He seemed to feel

24

particularly acutely the pain of people who were rejected and thrust to the margins of society. The strength and passion with which he loved the poor made him want to remake the world. From deep inside himself he felt that true happiness was impossible while people were excluded or made to feel worthless. He wanted the world to be a place with no outsiders; everybody was to be loved and to feel that they belonged. Hence, as we have seen, friars were to make their homes with lepers and Franciscan houses were to welcome thieves. The extensive woods of many regions formed a kind of underworld haunted by the poorest and most desperate members of society, such as fugitives, outcasts and outlaws. As early as the tenth century hermits had gone to live in the woods and had made contact with them, and by the time of Francis there was quite a tradition of the hermit life as open to these needy and occasionally violent people. So Francis, in telling his friars to turn nobody away, was consciously building on this tradition of welcoming even those regarded as enemies of society. For example, he instructed the friars at the hermitage above Borgo San Sepolcro to take bread and wine to the robbers hiding in the woods. Then, having won their trust, they were to ask them not to strike or injure anyone, and eventually they were to try to integrate them back into society.[26] It was the same with his feelings towards the poor whom he met himself. He was not only solicitous about their material welfare, but deeply distressed if they were subject to abuse. Thomas of Celano tells us that Francis took it very badly 'if he saw a poor person reproached or if he heard a curse hurled upon any creature by anyone'.[27]

What sort of prayer life nourished this deep social concern and ability to suffer with the suffering? Part of the answer has been given already, namely the way that Francis identified the poor in their vulnerability with Christ in his vulnerability. Indeed in the citation just given, which mentions the distress of Francis if he heard a poor person reproached, Thomas of Celano adds that Francis:

was accustomed to say, 'Who curses a poor man does an

injury to Christ, whose noble image he wears, the image of him who made himself poor for us in this world.' Frequently therefore, when he found the poor burdened down with wood or other things he offered his own shoulders to help them, though his shoulders were very weak.

Yet this was the same Francis who had previously been obsessed with good clothes and social standing. The rather shallow young man had grown into a person who physically and emotionally shared the distress of the poor and was always moved to do what he could to help them. In trying to understand how this transformation took place, perhaps we can unweave the strands of his spirituality a bit further.

Francis frequently meditated on the sufferings of Jesus on the cross, but it was how he meditated that made the difference. It is easy to make the cross a source of guilt. Here I think, for example, of those churches that display a large poster outside, showing a cross and hurling the angry question (often in red ink), 'Is it nothing to all you who pass by?' Francis, however, has a different approach, and one that is well rooted in scripture. If Francis were printing those same posters today his wording would, I believe, take some form of saying to us, 'See how much Christ loves you.' It was the combination of love and suffering in Jesus that moved Francis so powerfully. He thought often of the passion, sometimes with tears. Bonaventure tells us that 'The memory of Christ crucified was ever present in the depths of his heart . . . and he longed to be wholly transformed into him by the fire of love.'[28] At first glance this desire to become Christ might seem arrogant, blasphemous even. But note that Francis never claimed or aimed at any ontological identity, that is, he did not think himself to *be* Christ. Rather he aimed at conforming his emotions to those of Christ, and thus all the actions that would arise out of his inner disposition.

This emerges clearly in the story of the stigmata. In 1224 Francis went to the mountain of La Verna in the Appennine range where it runs through Tuscany. In the middle of September, during a forty-day period of intense prayer and fast-ing, Francis was caught up in a spiritual experience during which a vision left him permanently imprinted with the marks of the crucifixion. The *Little Flowers of St Francis* is a late and unreliable work,[29] but it is faithful to all that we know of Francis when it describes him during this experience as praying that he might share as fully as possible both the infinite love of Jesus for the world and the torment of his suffering on the cross.[30] The stigmata literally and metaphorically set the seal on twenty years of living through Christ. The significance of this for a spirituality of social concern lies in the way that Francis' desire to enter into Jesus' experience manifestly deepened his capacity to enter into the experiences of others. He was following the compassion of Jesus whom we find in the gospels so frequently identifying with the sick and needy, as well as those of low status (such as women) and even those who exploit others (such as Zacchaeus). By patterning himself on Jesus, Francis grew in his ability to see through other people's eyes and feel through their feelings; hence the strength of his compassion.

Any spirituality for justice and peace needs to be one which is similarly strong in compassion. Compassion depends on our sensitivity towards the world; it calls on us to develop our capacity for empathy. For Christians an obvious point of entry is meditation on the suffering love of Christ who alone is able to love each individual in the full knowledge of his or her circumstances. Part of Christ's suffering is loving while knowing the poverty, racism, illness, unemployment or loneliness that torments the person he loves. His love is such that he is present with them in their experience of life, knowing it from within better than they know it themselves. To love Christ is to love him in this suffering love for each person. Loving Christ therefore means going with him to share, as best we can, his love for people from within their world. It means sharing with him to the best of our ability his intimate understanding of all that oppresses people or causes suffering.

There is therefore no contradiction between growing in knowledge of Christ and growing in our understanding of the world. On the contrary, loving Christ seems to imply that we have a developing awareness of the crucial social questions of our day, such as apartheid in South Africa, urban poverty in Britain, capital punishment in the United States and the human cost of the arms race. Social evils such as these bring enormous suffering in their wake as they twist and crush the lives of countless individuals. To be able to share in Jesus' love for such people means being able to share to some extent in their horizons. In this sense compassion not only helps us co-operate with the movement of Christ's love, but it also fulfils us by increasing the capacity to relate to others without which there is no maturity. It is also worth noting that very few people are without some area of suffering in their lives. To grow in awareness of Christ's loving presence in other people's lives helps us grow in our awareness of him present in our own, and thus to come to terms with our own sources of pain.

Practically, what does compassion mean in our prayer life? One way forward is to take seriously the media as stimulus to prayer. It has become a cliché to complain about how depressing the news is. From newspaper, radio and TV we hear a daily catalogue of violence, oppression and natural disaster. I would suggest that our ability to turn this news into prayer is a crucial test of our ability to grow in compassion. If we allow the news to wash over us daily while we remain indifferent, then it will tend to have a hardening effect, because we will be accustoming ourselves to hear, read or see news of suffering without any response on our part. However, we can train ourselves to use these channels of news as channels of prayer. It is probably easiest with a newspaper, where we have the option of pausing when we come across an item of news which takes us into the reality of people's lives, then turning the item there and then into a brief intercessory prayer where we beg God to make himself known to the suffering people in this situation. I am aware, of course, that there are limits to what we can absorb. There is no virtue in *Weltschmerz*, a depression caused by our awareness of sufferings in the world (though realistically we must expect to get downcast about such things sometimes). That is why it makes

28

sense to specialize in two or three countries or contemporary social issues. This allows us to be selective by noting all that is important in our chosen fields, particularly where social pressure is reflected in known human tragedies.

Does such an approach lead us to passivity? The first reply to this is to say that prayer, in itself, is indeed a fundamental form of action. The second is that prayer builds up in us a disposition for action. We act out of what we know, particularly what we know in terms of feelings that we have assimilated. Where, like Francis, we have grown in compassion, like Francis we will have grown in our ability to act accordingly. Action will then arise out of some of our deepest beliefs and keenest intuitions. This is why it is important that our use of the media as prayer resources focuses not just on facts but on people. It is tempting to believe that what the public at large needs to change its thinking is more facts. More facts are indeed helpful, but they galvanize people less than the real stories of suffering people. To know that South Africa hangs an average of 150 people a year (nearly all black) is disturbing. But to read of or hear or see the witness of these victims, or of their loved ones, is to assimilate the truth at a greater depth, and to create in ourselves the possibility for a true compassion out of which we will act.

I believe that Francis' concern for peace is one example of how his compassion resulted in action, and to this I now turn.

A *spirituality of non-violence*

I suggested earlier that Francis and his first followers found that their spirituality was a subversive one, in that it helped them break through the conventions of the times. This becomes most obvious in their espousal of non-violence. They lived at a period when the carrying of knives and swords was common, and when local communities had the expectation that every able-bodied man would take up arms if instructed to do so by their leaders. On top of that, Italy was, of course, a very macho society: the land of the feud and the vendetta and of considerable male pride in physical power. Since then things may not have changed much; but in any case the thirteenth century was neither the place nor the time where it was easy to preach a gospel of peace and non-violence.

Yet this is what Francis and his followers did. Francis counted his preaching of peace as a divine mandate. In his Testament, Francis tells us, 'God revealed a form of greeting to me, telling me that we should say, "God give you peace." '31 And so Francis always began his sermons by praying for peace and by giving this greeting of peace.32 It was a message that Francis was as keen to preach by example. During a feud between bishop and mayor in Assisi, which threatened to divide the town, Francis reconciled the two by a deft piece of public liturgy in which he brought them together to hear the Franciscans sing (literally) the praises of forgiveness in words specially written by Francis. Francis could have the same effect on a larger scale. We know from a thirteenth-century chronicle that when Francis visited Bologna in 1222 or 1223 to preach, 'many noble clans, whose violence and long-standing feuds had raged with much bloodletting, were induced to agree to peace'.33 Francis also directly espoused non-violence. Citing Matthew 5:39 the Rule of 1221 tells the friars that they should offer no resistance to injury.34

Nor was this limited to friars. Men and women of all walks of life turned to him for inspiration, and only a small proportion of them were able or willing to become vowed religious living in community. He therefore encouraged the development of what was to become known as the Third Order, composed of people from all walks of life who tried to follow Christ after the manner of Francis. A rule was formalized for them in 1221 but this almost certainly draws on an earlier version. In the context of the times, the Third Order rule is quite startling, for regarding weapons it says that members of the Third Order 'are not to take up lethal weapons, or bear them about, against anybody'.35 Membership of the Third Order (or Penitents) grew quite quickly in Europe, and this provision regarding weapons had a powerful impact. According to the historian Paul Sabatier, in the early thirteenth century this witness to peace astonished Europe.[36] It did more than astonish: it also provoked controversy, because magistrates sometimes tried to force the Third Order men to bear arms. For a time the papacy defended the right of these followers of Francis not to do so.[37] This concern for peace was itself a form of action regarding a pressing need of the times. John Holland Smith comments that in preaching peace, Francis 'was speaking for, as well as to, the poor, to whom the constant wars and threats of war . . . meant nothing but additional burdens in a life already all but intolerably hard'.[38]

Even so, Francis was capable of getting swept up in that war fever of his time known as the crusades. In 1219 he went to join the army of the Fifth Crusade at Damietta in Egypt. What he found there was a profound shock, for this crusade, like others before it, was characterized by quarrelling, desire for booty and a ferocious hatred of Muslims.[39] In August Francis walked through the ranks of the Crusader army before an impending battle, saying that the fighting about to take place was contrary to God's will. The battle turned out to be a disaster for the Crusaders. Later Francis consciously risked his life by going from the Crusader army over to the Saracen lines, wanting to meet their leader, the Sultan of Egypt. At first he and his companion Illuminato were beaten, but they cried out 'Sultan' 'Sultan' (apparently all the Arabic that they knew). Their lives were spared and they were taken to the Sultan. Francis found himself before the hate-figure of the Crusaders, Sultan Malik al Kamil. For once dialogue – a courteous battle of wits about their respective religions – took the place of armed conflict. After several days of this Francis returned to the Crusaders, having refused expensive gifts from the Sultan but bearing a special pass which the Sultan had given him and which enabled him to visit the holy places in Palestine under Saracen control. There is something poignant about the presence of Francis in Jerusalem, able to visit through a peaceable spirit what was denied to the Crusaders through their preoccupation with conquest.

This dialogue between Francis and the Sultan of Egypt is

a remarkable lived parable in a time of conflict. Francis did not abandon his own most precious beliefs; nor, on the other hand, did he have any illusions about his co-religionists, the Crusaders. At the same time Francis accepted the Muslim Saracens as brothers under the skin. By going out to them he appeals to their mercy, and by arguing with them he assumes their rationality and basic goodwill. In other words, Francis refuses to accept the standard Christian projection of evil on to the Muslims. Such projection is an inherent human weakness, whereby we implicitly deny the darkness within us by loading it on to whoever is designated as 'the enemy'. Convinced of such people's inherent wickedness, we then wonder whether they are really human after all. Thomas Merton, whom I discuss in Chapter 5, once drew attention to how this process can be found in the talk of politico-military planners. It begins by assuming that the enemy is perverse and irrational, and proceeds to the conclusion that people like that understand nothing but force.[40] This was certainly the kind of ideology that Francis had to overcome in his own time. When he asked Cardinal Pelagius, the proud papal legate, for permission to go to the Sultan, the legate tried to dissuade him on the grounds that: 'Against such an enemy no good Christian should march except with lance in hand. No vice existed that was not found in the followers of the false prophet; they were treacherous, carnal, cruel, greedy, malicious, brainless, false-hearted.'[41] When, eventually, the Crusaders captured Damietta, they refused a Saracen offer of peace which would have given them Jerusalem, and they continued to pursue (unsuccessfully) a goal of outright conquest. So a Saracen attempt to achieve a negotiated peace was rebuffed. Perhaps we should also note at this point the restraint of the Sultan in resisting his advisers who told him to execute Francis and Illuminato. His restraint is the more remarkable considering the Crusader habit of catapulting severed Saracen heads into his camp.

The spark in the soul draws a person deeper into love of God and of the world, in a process of mutual enabling. And it is impossible to love others in this way while nourishing ancient hatreds and traditional grievances. Here Francis is a model for us. In his perception of the humanity of the enemy, in his honesty about his own side, and in his insistence on non-violence for Franciscans, Francis was, once again, subversive of the stereotypes and conventions of his day. If we want a spirituality of concern for the world around us, then we have to walk a similar path. In this context prayer can be a means of overcoming hostility towards our enemies. We need to incorporate into our prayers at least an occasional awareness of those regarded with hostility by our nation, our race or our class. We need to ask God to lead this enemy into whatever is right and fulfilling for them (and we need to refrain from telling God what that is). It is a good thing at the same time to incorporate into our prayers at such times a brief act of meditation, in which, before God, we simply see such people as individuals. As French Dominican Pierre Regamey puts it, 'It is perfectly possible for us to take a personal interest in them, by using a bit of imagination and visualizing what sort of persons they really are.'[42] And so as we hold them before God, we become aware of them as people like ourselves. This means seeing 'the Russians', for instance, not as an amorphous block hostile to ourselves but as lovers in each other's arms, parents doting on their children, babushkas (grannies) lighting candles before icons in churches; farmers and architects, coal-miners and secretaries; sick people in hospital, elderly people in homes; rock fans and chess enthusiasts. Thought of and prayed for in this way, it becomes less and less palatable to consider incinerating them. Jim Wallis, the American Evangelical pastor mentioned in Chapter 1, who works for peace, points out that as we pray we begin to see people as God sees them: 'Prayer undermines hostility and enables us to identify with another person. We bring them to mind in the presence of God, and our minds are changed toward them.'[43] This combination of intercession and meditation is one that can help us transcend national chauvinism and work for peace.

Finally more Christians need to ponder whether they should follow Francis in striving for a life of non-violence. As

a project for everybody, it is unrealistic. As a way of life
voluntarily adopted by some, it has great potential as an act
of witness and self-discipline. In his earlier life Francis was a
hot-blooded young man, capable of ordering people around
peremptorily, of flashes of anger and censorious judgment.
As the years pass he softens and becomes more and more
loving. This was the fruit of grace and of ascetic discipline.
In this latter respect, his non-violent approach to life played
its part in liberating him. He realized how violence could be
rooted in our opinions of others, and that in this respect words
could be as deadly as weapons. So he hated hearing his
followers run one another down. He wanted them to avoid
quarrels and a contentious spirit, and to be 'gentle, peaceful,
and unassuming, courteous and humble'.[44] There is, as
Francis knew, a continuity between our inner life and our
contribution to the harmony of society. This commendation
of humility and peaceableness occurs in the Rule of 1223 and
in a sense it distils how he had tried to live for nearly twenty
years. If we can follow it ourselves, then this approach is one
which should help us break down suspiciousness, curb bigotry
and increase our ability to seek out the good that is in others.
Because he had lived this way, Francis was able to see the
truth about his fellow-Crusaders and to approach the Saracens. His personal spirituality gave him the means for a
realistic social involvement.

Those who wish to follow Francis in this respect might
consider making a vow of non-violence. It is probably best to
take such a vow for a specific period, such as a year, and to
renew it for another specified period. It can be taken alone
or in a group; at home or in church. A good text for such a
vow is provided by Pax Christi USA:

Recognising the violence in my own heart, yet trusting in
the goodness and mercy of God, I vow for one year to
practise the non-violence of Jesus who taught us in the
Sermon on the Mount: 'Blessed are the peacemakers, for
they shall be called the sons and daughters of God. . . You
have learned how it was said, You must love your neigh-

34

bour and hate your enemy. But I say to you, Love your enemies, and pray for those who persecute you. In this way you will be daughters and sons of your Creator in heaven.'

Before God the Creator and the Sanctifying Spirit, I vow to carry out in my life the love and example of Jesus:

- by striving for peace within myself and seeking to be a peacemaker in my daily life;
- by accepting suffering rather than inflicting it;
- by refusing to retaliate in the face of provocation and violence;
- by persevering in non-violence of tongue and heart;
- by living conscientiously and simply so that I do not deprive others of the means to live;
- by actively resisting evil and working non-violently to abolish war and the causes of war from my own heart and from the face of the earth.

God, I trust in your sustaining love and believe that just as you give me the grace and desire to offer this, so you will also bestow abundant grace to fulfil it.

The spirit of this vow is very much in keeping with the discipline that Francis sought for himself and his followers. As such it is capable of leading us into a deepening commitment towards the needs of our suffering and strife-torn world.

I hope that I have shown how we can learn from Francis some of the components that can go towards making a spirituality for justice and peace. I have drawn the following lessons from Francis. First that to see God as revealing himself in dispossession will lead us towards the poor and help us to play our part in making them visible. Second that compassion is crucial and depends on our growing ability to see through the eyes of those who are suffering. Third and finally that non-violence of thought and action, word and deed can undergird our own approach just as it undergirded that of Francis of Assisi.

Some people may object that love of God is timeless, and that to relate spirituality to our times in this way is essentially a mistake. I would not agree with this analysis. Indeed one of the strengths of Francis' kenotic approach, with its stress on God's self-emptying in Jesus, is its strong implicit reminder that the incarnation took place precisely because God felt the world could not be left as it was. Through Jesus, God invites us to continue this work of rescuing the world from its folly.

Francis himself reflected the needs and pressures of his times. One of the reasons Franciscan spirituality succeeded was its accessibility to ordinary people. As one scholar comments, Franciscan spirituality was part of a medieval movement which affected many segments of society previously untouched: 'Serious religious aspiration could become, really for the first time in the Middle Ages, *popular* and accessible to peasants, married men and women, and others who fell outside the élitist vision of medieval monasticism.'[45] We need a similar development in spirituality in the late twentieth century, this time one that can show to the many people concerned about the fate of our planet how strong the links are between God's love and their concerns.

1   Eloi Leclerc, *Canticle of the Creatures: symbols of union* (Chicago, 1977), p. 137.
2   Lester K. Little, *Religious Poverty and the Profit Economy in Western Europe* (London, 1978), p. 22.
3   ibid., pp. 8–18.
4   ibid., pp. 36–9.
5   Rosalind Brooke, *The Coming of the Friars* (London, 1975), p. 112.
6   1 Cel. 2 in Marion A. Habig (ed.), *St Francis of Assisi: writings and early biographies* (Chicago, 1972), p. 230. This work is subsequently abbreviated to FO. I follow convention in abbreviating the First Life of St Francis by Thomas of Celano as 1 Cel., the Second as 2 Cel.
7   1 Cel. 103; FO, p. 318.
8   The Testament of St Francis, FO, p. 67.
9   Letter to All Clerics, FO, p. 101; see also The Admonitions, FO, p. 78.
10 Letter to All the Faithful, FO, p. 93.
11 FO, p. 61.
12 FO, pp. 680–1.
13 1 Cel. 17, FO, p. 242.

14 ibid; also Three Companions 12, FO, p. 901.
15 1 Cel. 17, FO, p. 243.
16 FO, p. 67.
17 ibid., p. 39.
18 ibid., p. 38.
19 ibid., p. 262; emphasis added.
20 ibid., p. 691.
21 1 Cel. 83, FO, p. 432.
22 Leonardo Boff, *St Francis: a model for human liberation* (London, 1985), p. 76.
23 Walter Brueggemann, *The Prophetic Imagination* (Philadelphia, 1978), pp. 32–43.
24 ibid., p. 21.
25 Jose Miguez Bonino, *Towards a Christian Political Ethics* (London, 1983), p. 131.
26 Mirror of Perfection 66, FO, p. 292. For an account of hermitages in relation to the marginalized people of society, see Thomas Merton, *Contemplation in a World of Action* (London, 1971), pp. 261–3.
27 1 Cel. 76, FO, p. 292.
28 FO, p. 699. For Francis' tears see 2 Cel. 11, p. 371.
29 John Fleming, *An Introduction to the Franciscan Literature of the Middle Ages* (Chicago, 1977), pp. 59–62.
30 FO, pp. 1448–9.
31 ibid., p. 68.
32 1 Cel. 23, FO, p. 248.
33 Archdeacon Thomas of Spalato in Brooke, op. cit., p. 136.
34 FO, p. 42.
35 ibid., p. 171.
36 Paul Sabatier, *Life of St Francis of Assisi* (London, 1922), p. 267.
37 Father Cuthbert, OSFC, *Life of St Francis of Assisi* (London, 1917), p. 341.
38 John Holland Smith, *Francis of Assisi* (London, 1972), p. 165.
39 See Steven Runciman, *A History of the Crusades*, vol. 3 (Cambridge, 1955), pp. 150–70; also Arnaldo Fortini, *Francis of Assisi* (New York, 1981), pp. 397–439.
40 Thomas Merton, *Thomas Merton on Peace* (London, 1976), p. 147.
41 Fortini, op. cit., p. 426.
42 Pierre Regamey, *Non-Violence and the Christian Conscience* (London, 1966), p. 179.
43 Jim Wallis (ed.), *Waging Peace* (San Francisco, 1982), p. 197.
44 FO, p. 60.
45 Fleming, op. cit., p. 18.

3

Meister Eckhart and God the Ground of Our Being

Meister Eckhart was born around the year 1260, less than forty years after the death of Francis of Assisi. Eckhart became a Dominican friar, and thus embraced the religious life in the same way as Francis. Yet despite these similarities there could scarcely be a greater contrast than these two influential medieval figures. Francis, as we have seen, frequently showed concern about the pressing social issues of his day, and acted directly to help the poor. From what we know of Eckhart, he showed little overt interest in the problems of society – though, as we shall see, what he taught had revolutionary implications and indicates a mind perceptively aware of the deeper issues of his day. Francis left little by way of writings, and was a doer rather than a thinker. Eckhart left a substantial body of written works, and possessed a speculative and keenly-honed mind. Francis sought God through the beauty of nature and through the power of images. Eckhart taught that in seeking God, images and the material world must be left behind. Francis stressed the power of love; Eckhart taught the power of the rightly-directed intellect. Finally, while there is a richness of biographical material about Francis, we know only the scant details of Eckhart's life. Even his first name is uncertain, though he was probably called Johannes.

Meister Eckhart's influence has been enormous. In his own time Eckhart was a formative influence in a movement of Rhineland mysticism that carried on for over a century after his death. His teaching on each person's direct relationship with God sank deep in German consciousness and came to the surface again in the Reformation; indeed we know that

Luther was influenced by the writings of Eckhart's pupil John Tauler (*c.* 1300–1361) and may have read Eckhart directly. The German philosopher G. W. F. Hegel (1770–1831) cited Eckhart in support of his own theories. In our own century Eckhart has influenced the thinking of another philosopher, Martin Heidegger, and the psychologist C. G. Jung, who wrote that in his reading during one difficult period, 'only in Meister Eckhart did I feel the breath of life'.[1] More recently Eckhart's teaching on God, the world and human consciousness as one integrated whole has been foundational for the new school of creation-centred spirituality, as expounded by Matthew Fox.

Eckhart was born in the Thuringia area of Germany around 1260 and joined the Dominicans somewhere between the ages of fifteen and seventeen. He studied at the University of Paris and at the Dominican theological school in Cologne. The twenty years between 1293 and 1313 saw him alternate between teaching in Paris and serving as a religious superior in Germany. It is a measure of Eckhart's stature among his fellow friars that in 1303 he was elected the first provincial minister of their newly-founded Saxon province, which included forty-seven priories and stretched from his native Thuringia to the Netherlands.[2] In 1313 he moved to Strasbourg where he taught theology and served as prior. Strasbourg was a prominent city both commercially and religiously. Many religious orders had houses both in and around Strasbourg. Eckhart became a well-known preacher and spiritual director, a role that continued when around 1322 he moved up the Rhine to Cologne where he became Dominican master of studies. In Cologne, however, disaster awaited, for in 1326 the Archbishop of Cologne began investigating Eckhart on suspicion of heresy. The case was referred to the pope at Avignon where Eckhart went to defend himself. In March 1329 Pope John XXII issued a bull condemning seventeen of Eckhart's propositions and putting eleven others under suspicion. Eckhart, perhaps fortunately, did not live to hear the judgment. He died in late 1327 or early 1328, probably at the Dominican priory in Avignon. There is a widespread belief today that the condemnation was wrong and possibly motivated by rivalry and by fear of Eckhart's influence on lay people in general and on women in particular. He brought such people new hope and a new vision of life at a time when vested interests in the church were deeply suspicious of anything which empowered lay people.

An outline of Eckhart's spirituality

It is a daunting task to try and give a thumbnail sketch of Eckhart's teaching, available to us from transcriptions of his sermons and talks, and from his biblical commentaries. He was a daringly original thinker who delighted in paradox. His style is often opaque. In an effort to convey what he meant both Eckhart and his commentators were driven to metaphors such as 'the trackless void of the Godhead' and 'the fathomless abyss of the soul'. Yet Eckhart has much to teach us about spiritual life in relation to the search for justice and peace, and we must summarize what he has to say in order to unpack what he has to offer. The following should be taken as no more than a sketch. His writings are substantial and complex. So the reader should be aware that in condensing and systematizing I have inevitably simplified what is complex and subtle.

It is probably easier to understand Eckhart if it is borne in mind that there is a parallelism in his accounts of divine nature and human nature. Divine nature has an aspect that is known, and another that is hidden and can never be directly known. So too, human nature has an aspect that can be known and another which is hidden. In divine nature it is the Godhead that is hidden. The Godhead is full of surging life, and in the first stage of creation (*bullitio*) emanates the Trinity. In the next stage of creation (*ebullitio*) this life pours through the Trinity in a fresh act of giving birth to the world, through which the divine life becomes known in space and time. In a further development the Son becomes incarnate, and God enters history. However the Godhead, or divine primal ground, remains unknown in itself even although it is the underlying reality of everything that exists.

As with divine nature, so too with human nature, which Eckhart describes in terms of the intellect. With each person there is an aspect that can be known. I know myself as a person who senses the world: I see, taste, touch, smell. I am also a person who thinks in ideas and images: I form concepts; I feel emotions – and show them. In such ways I know myself, and become known by other people. But although each of us could say this sort of thing about ourselves, on reflection there is an aspect of ourselves that we do not know. Sometimes we think of this aspect of ourselves as our hidden emotional life (influenced of course by Freud). We are uncomfortably aware of hidden forces, hidden longings, hidden feelings at work in our lives in a process of constant change. But Eckhart was pointing us beyond even this, to the self-consciousness which sustains even our hidden emotional lives. This sense of being present to ourselves is a kind of foundation which enables all kinds of other knowledge. But when we try to formulate *what* it means to be a person in this way, we can never adequately define it. Eckhart gave this hidden area of human identity many names, but I will use only one of these. He called it the 'power in the soul'. The power in the soul is not any particular state of self-consciousness, such as analytical thought, or emotional feeling, or sense awareness. It is rather what enables us to have such forms of self-consciousness. It is what bears us along – just as the Godhead bears the Trinity.

There are then two unknown grounds of being, the divine and the human, and the human one is a reflection of the divine. Eckhart was not simply being inventive here. The question of what it means for human nature to be made in the image of God (Gen. 1:26–27; cf. Rom. 8:29; Col. 3:10) is one that has fascinated Jews and Christians for centuries. In our own times Karl Rahner has some conclusions about human nature similar to Eckhart's. Rahner points to how humans are limitless in their horizons, in the sense that they are always able to go beyond present knowledge of everything

– including themselves. 'Every answer is always just the beginning of a new question.'[3] To know God is not like knowing an object from the outside; it is more like this experience of our own open-endedness, of our ability always to think afresh about something or feel differently. Once we begin to wonder where this endless human capacity comes from we become conscious, says Rahner, that human nature is indefinable, and we find ourselves facing 'the sea of infinite mystery'.[4] Where does this power always to think, and ask, and desire and seek come from? If we ask this question, we find ourselves delving into the depths of human consciousness, until we are facing that hidden power of which Eckhart speaks. It enables all conscious thought and analysis, but is itself beyond all conscious thought and analysis. It is a silent, luminous presence within. The only parallel we know is God, which is why Rahner speaks of the mystery of our own transcendence leading us to the mystery of God. Such a power within us can only be explained by reference to a similar, infinitely greater power: God. According to Eckhart this power is sustained by God and is in God's image. The hidden depths of divine consciousness make possible the hidden depths of human consciousness. As Eckhart says himself, 'Here God's ground is my ground and my ground is God's ground.'[5] We are rarely aware of this power in the soul, because we are usually absorbed in what Eckhart calls lower levels of intellect – with what we can see or hear or taste; with images; with feelings; with puzzling about this or that.

However Eckhart reminds us that while we cannot directly know this hidden source of our innermost life, we can be in touch with it, in a way that will allow its influence to permeate us. He uses the example of a spring of water covered by loads of earth; once uncovered it will bubble up anew with fresh water. This is like the preoccupations of our existence, which so crowd our consciousness that there is little or no awareness of the hidden power on which our consciousness itself depends. Once, however, we detach ourselves from these preoccupations and become open to the ground of our being, its influence will be felt throughout our lives. And because that ground of being is open to the infinity of God himself, who sustains us, the soul that frees itself from preoccupation with other things will become increasingly aware of God. Thus the way to fullness of human being is not the accumulation of possessions, the accretion of power or the expansion of knowledge: it is the ability to detach ourselves from these and turn towards God present within us. Eckhart teaches us that our recovery of this presence leads us to the true centre of our being and allows us to live out of our centre. It is a process of deepening.

What does Eckhart mean by 'detachment' in this way? He wants us to pray in a way that allows us to leave behind ideas both about ourselves and about God. Ideas about ourselves because it is part of the human condition to spend a lot of our thinking time and emotional energy on fitting the universe around our own needs and self-image. We are constantly drawing a mental picture with ourselves at the centre, and even prayer can be sucked into this process. Eckhart was seeking a balance in which we could find freedom to respond to God through consciously setting aside all the thoughts and images which crowd our mind: thoughts of status and prestige, of roles and conflict, of our own needs and the needs of others. In singleness of intent we need to still this mental marketplace and place ourselves naked, silent and attentive before God. And in commending this, Eckhart was not commending so much a method of prayer as an attitude of life. He wanted us to live in a way that allowed us to let go of preoccupations not only in times of set prayer but in the rush of living itself, though we might observe that our ability to do this in prayer will enhance our ability to do this in the ebb and flow of life.

What could it mean though, to carry this detachment into life? From a passive point of view it means a balanced acceptance of the hurts and slights that come our way. This does not mean becoming a doormat. All of us, however, have had the experience of wasting emotional energy fussing about things said or done to us which have slighted our self-importance or offended us, when really we could have let them pass.

Passive detachment can also help us come to terms with developments beyond our control, such as growing older. From an active point of view, detachment calls on us to create space between ourselves and the most important areas of our lives. Again this does not mean that we stop (for example) taking seriously our gifts or our social obligations. But it does mean seeking to create some emotional space between ourselves and such things, not being so bound up in them that they absorb the whole of our identity. Without some detachment we will never recover access to the power in the soul, the ground of our being as persons. We will be living out of the shallows.

Eckhart also wants us to incorporate into our spirituality a willingness sometimes to leave behind our ideas about God as well. He wants us to come to God abandoning all our preconceptions about God: all our images, doctrine, tradition, discursive thinking and so on, and simply to wait in the darkness of trust and hope for God to reveal himself to us in that space where our own hidden ground of being merges into his. This willingness to let go of our understanding of God is necessary because of our tendency to make God in our own image. It is also necessary if we are to move beyond our rational, analytical mind to the ground of consciousness itself. For those willing to do this, for those who pursue detachment, says Eckhart, God will make himself known as presence. Here we find ourselves, as so often with mystical experience, trying to express the inexpressible. He himself uses the metaphor of birth. Those who are able to rid themselves of images will find that God gives birth to the Son in them. The love exchanged in silence between each person and God is absorbed by God into the love between the Father and the Son. Sometimes Eckhart also speaks of a breakthrough (his word) in which the soul is united to the Godhead.[6]

I realize that here we are straining the limits of language and perhaps of faith. But I think it is possible to give a broader content to what Eckhart is saying. If we take our faith seriously, then we will sometimes find ourselves asking

the question, 'How can we be open to the influence of God?'
Eckhart's answer uses the experience of mystical union but
at the same time broadens this out to apply to men and
women of all walks of life. Openness to God is not the preserve
of some kind of spiritual élite. It is the fundamental constitu-
ent of Christian growth, and Eckhart is trying to help us
establish conditions that will encourage such openness. So it
is important to note that behind the metaphors of hidden
grounds of being, of giving birth and of breakthrough there
lies his conviction that every person has a built-in capacity
for the experience of God's presence within them. And indeed
Eckhart notes that sometimes it is the most avowedly religious
people who have the greatest difficulty in opening themselves
up to God. They stuff themselves so full of ideas *about* God
that they cannot get beyond the ideas to God himself. They
mistake the signpost for the road.

The social significance of Eckhart's spirituality

What Eckhart has to offer us is not a method of prayer but
a fresh expression of how we can draw close to God in a way
that helps us take seriously the needs of society. His vision
offers important insights for Christians seeking to link their
faith and their commitment to social justice, and I think that
we can see this most clearly with regard to the linked problems of world poverty, consumerism and environmental
blight. I would like to look at these problems in some detail.
I believe they are made more serious by a changed understanding of human nature, and will explain why, before turning back to what Meister Eckhart has to teach us in this
context.

We live in a world with marked divisions between rich and
poor. For a long time this has taken the form of disparities
between wealthy countries and poverty-stricken ones, but
increasingly there now appears to be a dividing line within
nations as well. The last two decades have seen the emergence
of urban poverty on a disturbing scale in the cities of western

Europe and north America. You do not have to go to Bombay to find a shanty town. There is one in the heart of London – 'Cardboard City' – next to its South Bank arts complex, where some of the homeless have erected flimsy shelters. Mother Teresa visiting London's homeless said that she found conditions there as bad as in any city in the two-thirds world. In Paris the destitute sit begging at Métro entrances holding signs explaining their plight. In New York the city authorities house 15,000 homeless people every night in vast shelters. In Washington in the depths of winter every morning the police pick up the bodies of one or two people who have frozen to death the previous night.

This visible emergence of poverty has dramatized and driven home the extremes of our world. Now, more than ever, citizens of western nations can see how wealth and poverty, abundance and need, live side by side. Yet at the same time there seems to be no restraint in the western (and Japanese) appetite for personal consumption. At the time of writing Britain has gone through a consumer boom in which the country's total personal indebtedness has risen to a colossal £285 billion. In recent years the United States has become the world's largest debtor nation, because of its voracious appetite for imports, many of them consumer durables. Neither the plight of local poor on the streets nor the plight of the poor overseas has dampened the consumption of consumer goods by prosperous nations.

One consequence of this consumer boom has been a growing pollution of the earth and destruction of its natural environment. The nations of north-west Europe, for example, dump 3.5 million tonnes of industrial waste into the North Sea and Baltic Sea every year. To this total must be added another 15 million cubic feet of industrial waste contaminated with chemicals such as lead, cadmium, mercury, nickel, phosphorus and dioxins. Meanwhile the cities of the north-eastern United States are running out of answers to dispose of their rubbish. New York alone produces 26,000 tons a day for its rapidly-filling dump on Staten Island, and expects soon to be spending $500 million a year on getting rid of garbage.

Philadelphia has tried shipping its garbage to Africa, and finds that no one will take the highly toxic ash from its rubbish incinerators.

These three crucial contemporary issues – poverty, consumerism and the environment – are all interlinked. We live in times when compulsive consumption is creating deep-seated poverty and environmental despoliation on a massive scale. We need urgently to seek answers to these problems on the economic, political and scientific levels. Yet this will not be enough, because the spiritual aspect needs to be addressed as well. One of the reasons why a reckless consumer appetite can thrive is the widespread implicit view of human nature as destined to consume and to find satisfaction through purchasing power. The way we now use the word 'consumer' invests it with particular significance. Note, for instance, how the phrase 'consumer demand' conveys public opinion, for it indicates people's expressed wishes and priorities. Again we hear of particular policies or developments being 'consumer-led', with people's buying intentions becoming a political force. The same holds true of the rarer 'consumer boycott'. What consumers want is a powerful expression of public opinion. Less notice is taken of those shut out of the purchasing mode of self-expression, and questions are not often asked about who and what shapes the public perception of which goods and services are desirable. The purchasing prism is adopted when viewing many forms of public activity which were formally regarded as communal – use of sports centres, for example, or libraries. The question has shifted from what the community can afford for its citizens to the question of what individuals can afford to buy, or pay for. The emphasis is increasingly on creation of a private world where people buy and consume what they want, with no limits on what money can buy. It is in these ways that the desire to purchase is implicitly portrayed as central to human nature, and as giving meaning to life. A new understanding of human nature is emerging, and it is an understanding which encourages limitless consumption by consumer citizens.

This is a development that has been accelerating for several decades, but it has been given further impetus by the recent influence of neo-conservative thinking, with its stress on market forces. On this view the unimpeded functioning of the market is the best foundation for any society. The laws of supply and demand are said to give people what they want and the laws of competition and profit are said to root out inefficiency. A society must therefore allow the market to operate more or less unimpeded in all areas of life including education, health and the environment. People will get what they are prepared to pay for, and the market will deliver the goods. This brand of conservative thought seems curiously close to Marxism at times, since both believe in an economic answer to human needs. But the model of human nature implied in this hymn to market forces is a deeply disquieting one. We see, more clearly than ever, the view that the person is first and foremost a consumer. Society becomes the arena of competing bidders, with people getting what they are prepared to pay for. We may note that this view allows little room for concepts such as loyalty, public service, job satisfaction and sacrifice. (It may also go some way to explaining why society sometimes indicates such vengeful attitudes to some of its most vulnerable citizens, such as those with AIDS, the unemployed, and the homeless; for they are precisely the people who cannot buy their way out of their difficulties, and therefore they do not count for much in society at large.) The idolization of the market that this current trend implies has also led to pressure for the abolition of controls on the market. For example, some exponents of market forces and free enterprise have pressed for (and in the United States sometimes won) the abolition of laws protecting areas of natural beauty or the homes of particular species from destructive commercial development.

It is against this backdrop that we must place Eckhart's vision of detachment and fulfilment. It is not enough to be criticizing the contemporary obsession with conspicuous consumption. The churches have been doing this, together with environmentalists and others, for over twenty years. Instead we need to help people grasp the possibilities of an alternative way of life, to understand what it might feel like. And more, such an alternative will have to *attract* – appeals to conscience are not enough. People are already showing signs of looking for such an alternative. The bleak picture of consumerism I have painted needs to be qualified by the growing interest in spirituality. People do sometimes seem to reach a point where endless consumption leaves them aware of the depths of their own need, an awareness that the infinity in them will only be matched by the infinity of God. Hence, in part, the renewed interest in prayer, in retreats and cursillos, in spiritual reading and direction.

This is where Eckhart's spirituality begins to seem so relevant to our present times. It will be remembered that earlier in this chapter I described the restlessness of the human spirit, always able to go on in the search for better understanding and more knowledge. Unfortunately this same restlessness often takes selfish forms, as we seek constantly to prove ourselves, to define ourselves, to establish ourselves as significant in our own eyes and in the eyes of others. The ever-moving human spirit often expresses itself in a hunger for possessions, status and experience. If Eckhart felt that people in his day were liable to be swallowed up by the images around them, how much truer is it of our own. We are, so to speak, 'all over the place'. Eckhart himself speaks of this condition as 'multiplicity' – a most suitable word for the bewildering variety of distracting images dangling before our consciousness all day long, in which we duly become engrossed. This process is reinforced by the current stress on market forces, with its belief that personal identity derives to a significant degree from purchasing ability. We believe that we become desirable through what we can purchase, or that we can define ourselves or prove ourselves in the eyes of others by possessions, status and personal services at our command.

In these ways many images and current ideology tell us that we grow as persons through the act of consuming goods and services. The process then begins to feed upon itself, because the process of distraction itself creates the need to consume. We become so used to having our attention filled up for us that we feel empty unless there are consumer goods or services to distract us. But in trying to find fulfilment and identity through what we can buy, we are literally trying to use the purchase of material things and services to meet an infinite human need. Of course there is another side to this picture. Such goods can often be a liberating factor. If I had to wash all my clothes by hand, using hot water I had boiled on a fire, which was made with wood I had gathered and chopped myself, then I might rightly feel that consumer goods would set me free. Moreover to people in eastern Europe and poorer countries of the two-thirds world, their lack of consumer goods is a potent symbol of their exclusion from the benefits of technological change. However, the purchase of consumer goods in the prosperous nations of the northern hemisphere now goes way beyond what liberates. In fact it now shows many signs of addiction. We are aware of the serious problem of drug addiction, notably in the United States, but the same pattern can be seen in other areas of personal satisfaction: addictiveness can be seen in alcohol, sex, possessions, food, status and power. Within many of our citizens there seems to be a deep unhappiness which demands to be assuaged by these things, which in themselves are not bad but which end up possessing us rather than liberating us. The pursuit of unnecessary consumer durables to satisfy a ceaseless yearning is simply part of this wider pattern of escape and addictiveness. Two characteristic features of addictiveness are present: first the search for a 'fix', an external source of satisfaction, that will temporarily quell the feelings of insecurity and need. Second the rising level of tolerance so that ever greater consumption is required to meet the need. This way we can exhaust the earth without plugging the gap. That perceptive fourteenth-century English mystic Julian of Norwich (who was influenced by Rhineland mysticism) recognized that people seeking fulfilment in material things are actually frustrating themselves of what they seek:

We have got to recognize the littleness of creation and to

see it for the nothing that it is before we can love and possess God who is uncreated. This is the reason why we have no ease of heart or soul, for we are seeking our rest in trivial things which cannot satisfy, and not seeking to know God, almighty, all-wise, all-good.[7]

Julian is not, of course, saying that creation is unimportant. The above quotation comes shortly after the famous passage in which something as small as a hazel-nut opens her eyes to the love and creativity of God. Rather Julian is saying that compared with the glory and love of God, everything else that we can possess seems small indeed. Or, as Jesus himself said, what profit has a person if the whole world is gained at the price of loss of soul (Mk 8:36)? It is as if the very abundance of consumer goods has exposed more sharply than ever the human need for a source of love which alone can sustain people through life.

Has there ever been a more appropriate time to rediscover the spirituality of detachment from images, and union with God? This is the spirituality of Eckhart, who reminds us that to live absorbed by desirable images is to lose touch with the source of life within us. Eckhart points us to the hidden ground of human being, in which the infinite human spirit meets and is borne by the infinity of God. Only by a rediscovery of this ground of the soul will we be able to cease our preoccupation with consumption. The first step is indeed to turn our mind away from material images. This needs to be followed by an inner stillness in which God can give his own gift of love, and work in our consciousness in a way which increasingly draws it into himself, where the endless striving and seeking finds an answer in the hidden exchange of love.

How does Eckhart show us the way? Here is a quotation from Sermon 68:

... nothing within us should be hidden: we should reveal it all to God and give it all to him. Whatever state we find ourselves in, whether in strength or in weakness, in joy or in sorrow, whatever we find ourselves attached to, we must abandon. In truth, if we reveal all to Him, He in return will reveal to us all that He has, in truth He will conceal absolutely nothing of all that He can perform: neither wisdom nor truth nor mystery nor divinity nor anything else.[8]

Here he is speaking of detachment and a divine–human mutual revelation. My understanding of this is that it is impossible to become detached without in some way becoming aware first of what we are attached to. There needs, therefore, to be in our lives some space in which we begin by prayerfully acknowledging whatever crowds in on us: anxieties about health or career; anger, jealousy, sexual needs; the faces of those whom we love; worries about the world; even particular thoughts about, or images of, God (as judge, redeemer, Trinity); in fact whatever insists on coming into our consciousness. Then, having acknowledged them before God, we need to let them fall away – repeatedly if necessary – and allow a pool of deep silence to grow within us, trusting that within that silence God as he is in himself, beyond all understanding, will make himself known as simple presence. Then, through God's own work, the deeper process of revealing will take place, in which in utter stillness and imagelessness our inner depths of being – our hidden ground – will be united in breakthrough with God's own hidden ground. Spiritual growth sometimes depends on our developing our inner freedom in this way. As Eckhart says in Sermon 68, 'as long as you want more and more, God cannot dwell or work in you. These things must always go out if God is to go in.'[9]

Clearly Eckhart expects some reciprocity between this inner process and our outer disposition. It would be impossible to pursue inner detachment sincerely without at the same time seeking a growing freedom from actual possessiveness. Indeed in Sermon 68 he speaks scornfully of those who think they can follow God 'in honour, riches and comfort'.[10] The detachment which is a prior condition of union with God thus influences our perceptions of our social position, our conduct as 'consumer' and our relations with other people. It is a process whereby we are not only learning to *let things go*, but also at the same time to *let things be*. How? Turning to the simple, imageless presence of God within us frees us at a deep level from attachments that feed the ego. William Johnston is a Jesuit writer on mysticism who lives in Japan and has studied Buddhism and Christianity for many years. He notes that:

> meditation that goes beyond thoughts and images to the inner core of silence is the arch-enemy of conscious and unconscious clinging . . . in the silence of a meditation that penetrates through layer after layer of consciousness, it liberates man from the tyranny of his internal fixations. It penetrates those murky subliminal depths and cleans them up. And then, liberated from clinging and possessiveness, I can see and relate to the other as other.[11]

Detachment thus means learning not to dominate or manipulate the natural world, people and events. Indeed Eckhart makes it perfectly clear that detachment grows until it becomes not so much a 'religious exercise' as a way of life. If only this approach could indeed take root, it could make an important contribution to a world in which some people are kept in poverty and whole landscapes despoliated in order to satisfy the appetite of others. As the Eckhart scholar Reiner Schurmann notes, the process of detachment is of great significance for our overall attitude to the world in which we live:

> It designates the attitude of a human who no longer regards objects and events according to their usefulness, but who accepts them in their autonomy. . . He who has learned how 'to let be' restores all things to their primitive freedom; he leaves all things to themselves. He has learned not to subject them to his projects. . .[12]

A spirituality producing such fruits would be highly relevant in a world racked by compulsive consumerism, poverty and exploitation of the environment. Such an approach changes the inner attitude which sees all things and all other people as material for our projects, an attitude which when carried over into action has disastrous effects on our world.

Detachment, of course, is not an end in itself. It is intended to create the conditions whereby God can draw us into himself. As Caputo puts it:

> To be poor in spirit is to completely strip ourselves, to 'divest' ourselves of our personal goals and desires, to empty out every vestige of self-love and self-will, not in order to replace them with higher goals and desires, but rather in order to 'let' something else – the impulse of God's own life within us – take over.[13]

This belief in the possibility of God somehow living through us, and of divine will refracted through us, is not exactly prominent in current Christian thinking. Yet Eckhart puts it in the strongest terms, saying, for example in Sermon 7, that through the birth of the Son in someone, God gives that person 'the essence and the nature and the substance and the wisdom and the joy and all that God has'.[14] This may seem a dangerously high-reaching claim, yet it is faithful to that aspect of Christian tradition which teaches that believers take on the features of Christ. The letter to the Ephesians contains the prayerful hope that God may:

> out of his infinite glory . . . give you the power through his Spirit for your hidden self to grow strong, so that Christ may live in your hearts through faith . . . until, knowing the love of Christ, which is beyond all knowledge, you are filled with the utter fullness of God. (Eph. 3:16–19)

Similarly in Galatians 2:20 Paul makes bold to say, 'I live now not my own life but with the life of Christ who lives in me.' And in 2 Corinthians 3:18 Paul uses the mirror image of which mystical theologians were to become very fond: he writes that the Spirit is at work in believers, so that 'we, with our unveiled faces reflecting like mirrors the brightness of the

Lord, all grow brighter and brighter as we are turned into the image that we reflect'.

Union with God has been understood in different ways in the history of spirituality. One way of viewing it is in terms of our conformity to the will of God. Our intentions, our actions, our perceptions, increasingly reflect our understanding of what God asks of us. We become united with God to the extent that in some sense our choices and actions are his. This too is extremely important for social justice, especially the linked problems of consumption, poverty and ecology. Union with God changes our perceptions of the world. Commenting on the passage quoted above from Sermon 7, Schurmann says that it refers to a development whereby 'Man's sensibility is sharpened to the point of recognizing God in all things'.[15] Union with God is a process which heightens our sensitivity to how everything proceeds from God. As we will see in Chapter 4, Evelyn Underhill refers to this as the 'universalizing' of our perceptions and will. Such an experience ends the self-absorption whereby we orient everything around ourselves, and in so doing fragment it. Instead we are given a glimpse of how everything is co-related and interacts through God's gift of being. This in turn enables us to perceive God at work in what we often mistakenly call the 'secular' world, as if God's world was contained in churches and chapels.

In fact one of the reasons Eckhart's approach attracts more and more people today is the way in which he offers us an understanding of God who escapes, as it were, the church. He calls on us to be detached from the traditional ways of understanding God, because all representations are ultimately inadequate. Eckhart assumes that we will be nourished in all the traditional ways: the sacraments, church art, formal prayer, liturgy and so on. He has many beautiful and pastorally wise things to say about the importance of confession, for example, and on the right reception of the Eucharist. But he balances all this with the advice that in some way we must become detached from these, in order to seek union with the God who is beyond all formal knowledge. And this detachment is one which helps carry us into union with God and

into the experience of God in everyday life. The seeking of
God through unknowing is a process which should give us
eyes more perceptive to God's work and presence. God is met
everywhere. Christians who take Eckhart seriously will be
more attuned to the prophetic side of religion, to a God who
works through the 'secular' events and developments of the
world as much as the sacred. This can open us up to God as
being found in our involvement in the turbulent and sometimes messy process of creation and re-creation, of growth
and change in a world where human freedom produces both
sin and love. In the Talks of Instruction given to younger
Dominican friars, Eckhart told them that 'if a man truly has
God with him, God is with him everywhere, in the street or
among people just as much as in church or in the desert or
in a cell'.[16] Eckhart recommends making God not so much
the constant focus of their attention as a permanent colouring
of their consciousness. This will enable people to expect God
to come to them out of the events, big and small, of life –
'they look around them to see where he whom they expect is
coming from'. For people with this state of mind, 'God would
shine forth as nakedly in the most worldly things as in the
most godly.'[17] We learn to see (so to speak) through the eyes
of God. We decreasingly view the world from the standpoint
of our self-assertive individuality. We increasingly see ourselves related in God to other people and to nature, linked
with him in loving them, and act freely in accordance with
what we thus know deep within ourselves.

Those who persevere in this way, until they enter into
union with God, will find themselves so shaped by God, says
Eckhart, that they come to share God's attributes such as
goodness and justice. The just person becomes justice; the
good person becomes goodness.[18] Here he is pointing to that
strange process of growth whereby we internalize what we
hold most deeply to be true. It is the difference, say between
stopping at a red light ('this is the law and I might collide
with another car if I ignored it') and stopping to help an
injured person ('how could I do otherwise?'). Deep within us
are beliefs and attitudes which can powerfully dispose us

towards action. Detachment helps us rediscover and reflect more clearly the image of God. But, Eckhart reminds us, this God is also the supreme meaning of goodness and justice. To be formed in God's image in the ground of our being is thus also to find our deepest attitudes and beliefs changed in a way that frees us to act for goodness and justice. Grace Jantzen has pointed out how for Eckhart, as indeed for many mystics, abandonment of the will allows a divine–human unity in which the human will unites with the divine. The human will does not conform to the divine will out of compulsion. Rather this alignment is made possible because the experience of union has brought the person to an integration and authenticity in which that person is more able freely to choose what is right and good. As Jantzen puts it:

> The intimate union with Christ is frequently spoken of in the New Testament in terms of the indwelling Holy Spirit, so that all actions become, while in one sense the authentic actions of the integrated individual, in another sense the outflowing of the divine life. 'It is no longer I who live, but Christ who lives in me,' says St Paul; yet he would be the first to say that it is in this new life in Christ that his actions are for the first time really his own, free from tyranny.[19]

Union with God thus bears fruit in our free actions in the world, and detachment sets in motion a process with important consequences for our role in society.

At this point the reader may well be saying, 'Yes, union with God is all very well, but it's only for spiritual giants – it's not the kind of thing an ordinary, struggling believer can think about.' Being an ordinary, struggling believer myself I would sympathize with such a statement – but strongly disagree with it. I think that one of the reasons mystics enjoy a growing readership is that they help ordinary people make sense of some of their own spiritual experiences. As Evelyn Underhill points out, mysticism is, generally, a 'communion of love' between God and the believer. Viewed this way we realize, she says:

that mysticism represents the very soul of religion; that it is, in fact, another name for that which is sometimes called 'the spiritual life'. . . Not only the act of contemplation, the vision or state of consciousness in which the soul of the great mystic realizes God, but many humbler and dimmer experiences of prayer, in which the little human spirit truly feels the presence of the Divine Spirit and Love, must be included in it . . . every human soul has a certain latent capacity for God.[20]

Eckhart points us towards that capacity, one with important social consequences when we begin to utilize it. Detachment is simply a clearing of the ground to allow God to make himself known. Union occurs when God comes into the space. This spiritual process is just as possible in the quiet of your sun-drenched sitting-room as in the gloom of a Gothic cloister.

Eckhart's metaphor of birth

The union with God that Eckhart is pointing us towards is one which he believes fits into a whole system of being. In the outline of his spirituality, I have described how he envisaged the Trinity emanating from the Godhead (*bullitio*) and the created order coming from the Trinity (*ebullitio*). Eckhart depicts a twofold process. In the first process creation flows out from God, beginning with the Trinity, which in turn makes possible the universe. In the second process creation then flows back into God, as persons turn to him and through detachment and union are reunited with the origin of all things. This is frequently described by him in images of birth. The birth of the Word (or the Son) in us enables union with God and thus becomes a second birth back into God. In this picture the whole of the universe is a living entity. Of itself it is nothing, for only God possesses being; the being of the universe derives from God. God sustains the world through his divine power and love. Sometimes Eckhart can sound fiercely anti-world, saying, for instance in Sermon 32b, that

'All creatures are too base to be able to reveal God'.[21] But his intent is not to detract from the glory of creation. He is concerned rather that it be seen in right perspective, as dependent upon one who is utterly beyond it. Thus this harsh statement about baseness is part of a passage which says God is without equal, transcending his creation analogously to the sun transcending a tree which it keeps alive, or like a painter whose skill creates a portrait. These are not hostile images but ones intended to bring us to a right perspective. Everything is linked to God in dependence on his being.

This theme of emanation and return reflects the influence of Neoplatonism on Eckhart. The Neoplatonist school believed in emanation of everything from a primal source, and fulfilment in return to that source. We find it hard to think in such terms today, although there are contemporary theologies which have resemblances to this, such as process theology and the work of Teilhard de Chardin. So is the form in which Eckhart articulates union with God of any use for us today? I believe that it is, and that it relates to the issues of poverty, consumer wealth and environmental problems. It links with a growing need felt today for new ways of understanding the relationship between God and the world. The United States theologian Sallie McFague says that 'the language used to express the relationship between God and the world needs revision . . . this revision must begin at the level of the imagination, in a "thought experiment", with metaphors and their accompanying concepts'.[22] She adds that contemporary Christian theology needs an organic, or mutualistic way of understanding the world, a model by which we can see that all that exists is interrelated and has an intrinsic worth. She feels that contemporary thinking, encouraged in part by religious tradition, has adopted a very different mechanistic perspective which thinks in terms of power, function and separation of entities.[23] What is needed is 'an appropriate language for our time', one which 'would support ways of understanding the God-world and human-world relationships as open, caring, inclusive, interdependent, changing, mutual and creative'.[24] Metaphor helps in this process because it uses something from the familiar and everyday aspects of life to describe our relationships. The best metaphors, as McFague notes, are those which 'are imaginative leaps across a distance . . . always giving both a shock and a shock of recognition'.[25] Through metaphor we can recognize something as true, seeing it that way for the first time, as its imaginative boldness seizes our attention and breaks through our previous understanding.

In line with this approach I want to suggest that one of the ways in which Eckhart's system 'works' is as metaphor. As Thomas O'Meara puts it, Eckhart shows that 'God's life is one of creative love pouring forth into Trinity, cosmos, spiritual selfhood, Incarnate head.'[26] This conceptual metaphor gives us a picture of God's nature, the material world, and human responsiveness in one umbilically linked system. Eckhart helps us understand God as vibrant with life – 'fecund' is a word he uses – endlessly expressing the divine nature through the created order. This is a God, who, in the words of Sermon 88, 'pours Himself out into all creatures, to each as much as it can take. . . This God loves all creatures equally and fills them with His being. And thus too, we should pour forth ourselves in love over all creatures.'[27] Here we do not have a picture of humankind lording it over creation, sharply distinguished from it in a relation of domination. Instead we have a picture of humankind sharing with the rest of the world the status of constantly being made by God's outpouring. We imitate God if we similarly pour ourselves out in love towards the world that God creates.

As a theologian and teacher, Eckhart believed that we must discover the God who is beyond all images; but as a pastor and preacher he used images boldly and imaginatively to convey a fuller understanding of God.[28] Perhaps it is not surprising that someone who urged detachment from images of God came up with fresh and insightful ones when he used them. And so we find that in addition to the conceptual metaphor of life surging forth from the Godhead there is the associated metaphor of God and persons as united in giving birth. Take, for example, Sermon 68: 'God's chief aim is giving birth. He is never content till He begets His Son in us. And the soul, too, is in no way content until the Son of God is born in her.'[29] Sometimes Eckhart links this birth of the Son in our soul with the begetting of the Son, using the birthing metaphor for both: 'God has ever been begetting His only-begotten Son and is giving birth to him now and eternally: and thus He lies in childbed like a woman who has given birth, in every good, outdrawn and indwelling soul.'[30]

It is interesting to note that there are parallels in the Bible. In Isaiah 42:14 God is described as 'groaning like a woman in labour', and in Isaiah 66:9 is described as the one who brings the womb to the point of delivery. Eckhart's use of images of birth speaks of ourselves and the world as reflecting, in our different ways, the divine fecundity. We are all three interlinked in a single fruitfulness: God, the soul, the material world. The metaphor of giving birth, and the broader metaphor of one interlinked system of fruitfulness coming from and returning to God, give a rich extra dimension to our prayer life and to our linked understanding of ourselves in relation to God and the world. The responses such a metaphor evoke are those of nurture and the thankful rejoicing we associate with birth. If we see ourselves as the place of divine birth-giving, the natural response is to become co-carers with God for the world which is, in itself, the fruit of the divine fecundity. And since in Eckhart's system there is no being outside God,[31] wasteful exploitation of nature begins to look like an offence against God herself, whose creative love bears all things in being.

The image of God that Eckhart offers us is also one of God who is giving birth in us. Birthing is a dynamic metaphor that speaks to us of a painful and joyful process of becoming, in which the new is borne out of the old. The birth which is spoken of is of God's presence made real in us. If we really believed that God was giving birth in us, then it would be impossible *not* to carry out in our actions all the love and joy and responsibility for the world that would come from that birth. The metaphor invites us to see *ourselves* as the place of hope, of new beginnings, of awareness and creativity. It is a metaphor with a rich resonance. It invites us to engage in creative action for change, arising out of what God is doing in us.

The process that begins with God's presence in us thus culminates in our becoming God's presence in the world. This is the contemporary equivalent of Eckhart's circle of emanation and return, and it is one that I believe is true to his own intent. God creates the world and then, through women and men who find that God's presence empowers them, God draws the world back into God's loving intentions. We could even say that such people become God's wider presence, shaping and reshaping the face of the earth which God's surging life has created and bears in being. God chooses to work through free beings. God's presence thus depends on sons and daughters who respond to divine love, making room for God in their lives by detachment and seeking union with God as the deepest truth within them.

Detachment and union lived: Dietrich Bonhoeffer

It seems appropriate at this point to ask if I can point to any examples of what I mean. In this respect I want to say something briefly about Dietrich Bonhoeffer. I am not, of course, citing him as giving answers to the particular complex of consumerism, wealth and ecology. I do however see him as an example of how detachment and union can free people to take seriously the social and political issues of their times.

Dietrich Bonhoeffer was born to prosperous and respected parents in Germany in 1906 (his father was a psychiatrist). He became a Lutheran pastor, and shortly after Hitler came to power Bonhoeffer became involved in opposition to him. Bonhoeffer joined others such as Martin Niemoeller in trying to halt the Protestant Churches' complicity with Nazism. They set up a Confessing Church. Ministers for this church were trained by Bonhoeffer in a small seminary at Finkenwalde in Pomerania. Bonhoeffer had been a pastor and university lecturer with a brilliant career ahead of him; at Finkenwalde he was a marginal figure in the life of the church, under threat of arrest by the Gestapo. After the closure of the seminary by the authorities Bonhoeffer went to teach in the United States in 1939. On arrival in New York, however, he went through a period of intense struggle as a result of which he chose to return to Germany to resist Hitler and face almost certain death. In the latter years of the war he became involved in a plot to kill Hitler, was imprisoned and executed in 1945, within sound of the gunfire of the advancing Allied armies.

The Rhineland mystical tradition left its mark on Lutheran spirituality. As a medieval Catholic priest, Eckhart was of course very different from Bonhoeffer, a twentieth-century Protestant pastor. But the Lutheran faith in which Bonhoeffer was brought up had been influenced by Rhineland mysticism's stress on the Christian's direct, unmediated experience of God, speaking deep within each person. For example, in one of his early sermons Bonhoeffer said:

> it takes daily courage to expose oneself to God's word and to allow oneself to be judged by it, it takes daily energy to delight in God's love ... What shall we do, in order to penetrate into this silence before God? ... Not one of us lives such a hectic life that he cannot spare the time ... to be still and let the silence gather round him, to stand in the presence of eternity and to let it speak, to enquire from it about our condition, and to gaze deep into himself and far out, beyond and above ... his soul begins to be replenished and revitalized and to receive strength, then he begins to know the eternal quiet which rests in God's love; stress and anxiety, hurry and restlessness, noise and clamour are stilled within him, he has become silent before God who is his help.[32]

In this sermon Bonhoeffer says that he is speaking from experience. It is not difficult to see this experience as similar to Eckhart's teaching on union with God, even though Bonhoeffer might not use the word 'union' itself.

His writings in the following years show a sustained grappling with self-will, a struggle for detachment; he was seeking a radical openness to and dependence on God. There is detachment in his prayer life, as the early sermon indicates. Perhaps the development of detachment in prayer enabled him to deepen his detachment when the challenge was to speak out as conscience told him, though he knew it would cost him his standing in the church. There was detachment in his ability to be faithful to his love of Germany while seeing through the sick nationalism that was being fostered there. There was detachment of a most costly kind when he left the safety of the United States. Finally there was detachment when he decided, after a painful struggle, to become involved in the plot, in the lying, deception and willingness to murder which it required of him. Although he realized that this was necessary, he was also clear that he was becoming involved in evil, and it was a very difficult process for him.[33] But he was strengthened throughout by his relationship with God, by his prayer. Prayer fed into life, detachment and union undergirded the commitment to action. Bonhoeffer shows us how the type of spirituality advocated by Eckhart can dispose us towards involvement in pressing social issues.

The sceptic might still object that spirituality does not necessarily have any power, even when a person does become involved in society. This begs many questions about power. However, one way of reply would be to point to Eckhart's own influence. He lived at a time when institutional religion was showing many signs of oppressive corruption. For example, there was growing stress on wealth as an escape from the consequences of sin in purgatory, since those with money could purchase indulgences either directly or by pilgrimages or endowments, or by arranging for vast numbers of masses to be said for them. At the same time the religious cult was becoming increasingly complex and ornate, and religious discourse was becoming complicated and abstruse; both these developments excluded lay people from involvement in the life of the church, which became more than ever the preserve of the clergy. God too began to seem increasingly remote, reached through a realm of saints who, as God's friends, had an influence with God that ordinary mortals could never have, the saints being able to placate God and win favours from him. At the same time the church was becoming increasingly involved in bitter struggles between nations and dynasties, compromising its integrity

Seen against this backdrop Eckhart's teaching seems revolutionary. It is significant that he preached in the vernacular, one of the first to do so; this made him one of the founding figures of German literature. It is significant too that he preached particularly to communities of women. Women were among the most marginalized of the lay people at this time, and their formation of religious communities was one of the few outlets for women of talent and ability. Even so the institutional church regarded them with suspicion. When Eckhart preached to women like this he treated them as people capable of grasping profound and subtle points. He must have gravely alarmed the authorities, and his preaching to women and to lay people in general was probably one of the reasons for his denunciation as a heretic. At this time of a remote God more available to the rich, Eckhart was telling people about a God who made himself known as presence in each God-seeking person.

At this time too, of complicated ceremonial and of attempts to mollify God, Eckhart was telling people that obsession with method could take them further from God rather than closer. And at this time when the church was allied with the rich, Eckhart was preaching that rich and poor were alike in bearing the divine image. The historian Richard Southern comments: 'Eckhart's depreciation of external practices, rules, disciplines and vows, his incipient nihilism, his insistence that the soul's joys could be fulfilled in the world and in the market-place no less than in church or in the cloister, cut across the carefully-articulated system of the medieval church. . .'[34] His ideas took root in German consciousness until, with the work of others, they burst forth in the Reformation. Southern concludes that 'The people whom he roused could never again be kept in order, the thoughts he suggested could never be suppressed, and Europe could never be the same again.'[35]

All in all, quite a remarkable achievement for someone who was speaking and writing about the relationship of the person to God. I hope that I have indicated how his spirituality can have a transforming effect today. His understanding of detachment from material things and union with God could help change the climate of public opinion which favours head-long consumerism, rich–poor divisions and ecological problems. Much of the spirituality taught in church circles today proceeds from an image-rich Ignatian tradition. It looks as if it is time to balance this with Eckhart's teaching on detachment and the inner presence of God.

1   C. J. Jung, *Memories, Dreams, Reflections* (London, 1983), p. 87. See also Jung's examination of Eckhart's ideas in Jung, *The Collected Works*, vol. 6, *Psychological Types* (London, 1971), pp. 241–58.
2   Thomas O'Meara, 'The presence of Meister Eckhart', *Thomist*, vol. 42, no. 2 (April 1978), p. 175. This special issue on Eckhart is subsequently cited as *Thomist*.
3   Karl Rahner, *Foundations of Christian Faith* (London, 1978), p. 32.
4   ibid., pp. 21–2.
5   M. O'C. Walshe (ed. and tr.), *Meister Eckhart: sermons and treatises*, vol. 1, p. 117 (Sermon 13b). This three-volume work is subsequently cited as Walshe, vol. 1 (London and Dulverton, 1979); vols 2 and 3 (Shaftesbury, 1987).
6   For a careful treatment of this difficult area of Eckhart's thought, see John D. Caputo, 'Fundamental themes in Meister Eckhart's mysticism', *Thomist*, pp. 217–23.
7   Julian of Norwich, *Revelations of Divine Love* (Harmondsworth, 1966), p. 68.
8   Walshe, vol. 2, pp. 160–1.
9   ibid., p. 158.
10 ibid., p. 162.
11 William Johnston, *Silent Music* (London, 1974), p. 143.
12 Reiner Schurmann, *Meister Eckhart: mystic and philosopher* (Bloomington and London, 1978), p. 16.
13 Caputo, op. cit., p. 201.
14 Walshe, vol. 1, p. 67.
15 Schurmann, op. cit., p. 170.
16 Walshe, vol. 3, p. 16.

17 ibid., p. 20.
18 ibid., pp. 61–3, 71, 86 (Book of Divine Comfort).
19 Grace Jantzen, 'Human autonomy in the body of God' in A. Kee and
    E. T. Long (eds), *Being and Truth* (London, 1986), p. 193. (Jantzen in
    accompanying footnotes refers to Gal. 2:20; 5:1 and 5:13.)
20 Evelyn Underhill, *The Mystics of the Church* (n.d.), pp. 10–11.
21 Walshe, vol. 1, p. 243.
22 Sallie McFague, *Models of God* (London, 1987), p. 20.
23 ibid., pp. 11–12.
24 ibid., p. 14.
25 ibid., p. 35.
26 O'Meara, op. cit., p. 179.
27 Walshe, vol. 2, p. 157.
28 Frank Tobin, *Meister Eckhart: thought and language* (Philadelphia, 1986),
    p. 81.
29 Walshe, vol. 2, p. 157.
30 ibid., p. 281 (Sermon 68).
31 Tobin, op. cit., p. 39.
32 Quoted in Mary Bosanquet, *Bonhoeffer: true patriot* (London, 1978),
    p. 71. This book was originally published as *The Life and Death of
    Dietrich Bonhoeffer*.
33 ibid., pp. 219–20.
34 R. W. Southern, *Medieval Humanism* (Oxford, 1970), p. 25.
35 ibid., p. 26.

4

Evelyn Underhill and God in the Present

In a curious way it can be easier to believe in a fourteenth-century prophet than in a twentieth-century one. With someone like Eckhart we readily remember how the intellectual and social horizons in his day differed from our own, and we make appropriate allowances. With someone like Evelyn Underhill this becomes more difficult. She lived close enough to our own time for us to expect that she ought to share our perspectives and our insights. Yet she was born in 1875 into a world very different from that of the late twentieth century: the comfortable, confident world of the Victorian middle classes. Her father was a lawyer who was eventually knighted. Her husband Hubert Stuart Moore was similarly a lawyer. The expectations of her day would have been satisfied if she had been a good wife, content with the smooth running of her household and assisting the progress of her husband's career. The times were not generally conducive to female advancement. We ought to remember, for instance, that she was forty-three before she could vote (in the General Election of December 1918), women having been enfranchised by parliament earlier that year. And she was thirty-one before her parents allowed her to marry Hubert, who had been courting her for many years.

We will also get a better sense of Evelyn Underhill's achievements if we remember the restrictions on women's activity in the church. Evelyn Underhill had no aspirations to be ordained, but the restrictions on work by women in the Church of England at that time gives the measure of how she triumphed over circumstances. Women's ministry was largely

confined to the work of nuns and deaconesses. When one of
the first deaconesses was ordained in Bedford in 1869 her
bishop told her that 'setting aside all unwomanly usurpation
of authority in the Church' she should 'seek to edify the souls
of Christ's people in the faith'.[1] Deaconesses were largely
confined to work with women and children. They were
allowed to conduct worship only at informal services which
were usually held on weekdays. Not until 1941 were deaconesses legally allowed to lead and preach at morning and
evening prayer; preaching at the Eucharist was specifically
forbidden until 1973.[2] Another indication of the temper of the
times was the fate of lay women's proposed participation in
the National Mission of Repentance and Hope called by the
Archbishop of Canterbury, Randall Davidson, in 1916. The
Bishop of London had agreed to a proposal that lay women
should speak in church at meetings of women and girls,
provided that they did not claim authority by speaking from
pulpit, lectern or chancel steps. This modest proposal created
such a storm of controversy that the bishop hastily changed
his mind.

Among the more bizarre statements about women was that
of the Dean of Canterbury, the Very Revd Henry Wace, who
said in Convocation in 1919 that differences 'not only in the
physical but also psychical constitution of women' made them
unsuitable for regular public preaching. His statement
ignored the fact that for much of the preceding four years
women had been operating heavy machinery in munitions
factories, keeping them going day and night. They had also
been nursing badly wounded men on the front, sometimes
under bombardment. But his misgivings about the female
constitution were clearly shared by others: in 1920 the Lam-
beth Conference asked a female physician, Dr Letitia Fairfield, to report privately on the medical aspects of women
and lay ministries. Her report strongly affirmed the physical
capabilities of women; in fact she told the bishops that it was
men's superstitions about menstruation which was blocking
women's ministry, the continuing, partly subconscious belief
in women's 'ceremonial uncleanness'. It was, she said, neither

'lack of spiritual worth' nor 'mental quality' which was the real reason for the church's discrimination against women.[3]

This was the kind of background that Evelyn Underhill simply transcended in her different roles: by the time of her death in 1941 she had become probably the foremost lay theologian in the country. She was fascinated by the relationship of the eternal, unseen world to this one, and at first tried to tackle this theme in three novels published between 1904 and 1909. But in 1908 she began a programme of self-directed research which bore fruit in 1911 in her book, *Mysticism*. It was a huge success, being reprinted eighteen times between then and 1960. After 1911 a stream of books and articles appeared, usually about mysticism, prayer, spirituality or liturgy; but she also wrote poetry and biography, and brought out critical editions of medieval mysticism, such as *The Cloud of Unknowing* and works by van Ruysbroeck and Walter Hilton. She helped create a renewed interest in mysticism and its lessons for the contemporary world.

Evelyn Underhill's activities spread far beyond writing. She became a sought-after counsellor, spiritual director and retreat-giver, taking up to eight retreats a year. She was much in demand to speak at conferences, including clergy conferences, and at meetings on social and political issues. She broadcast a series of talks on the BBC in 1931, and was invited back to broadcast in 1936. Part of Underhill's amazing talent was her ability to write both for simple people and for the scholarly. Her academic recognition included becoming a Fellow of King's College London (where she had studied) and an honorary doctor of divinity of Aberdeen University. She was a friend of some of the leading writers of her day, such as the poets Rabindranath Tagore and T. S. Eliot.

When she began writing Underhill was not a Christian in any conventional sense. For several years after leaving school she counted herself an atheist, and even when she began to rediscover faith she sat lightly at first to church and doctrine. We hear her feelings spoken through a character in her first novel, *The Grey World* (1904), who says that at his school 'both cricket and Latin prose were serious things; but the soul was only mentioned on Sundays, and then in a purely official manner'. Her distaste for formal religion of the Anglican variety occurs again in this novel, when another character comments that 'It seems natural to the Englishman to behave coldly and correctly to his God.'⁴ However in the ten years following the publication of *Mysticism* Underhill became increasingly concerned to live out personally the challenge to love, spiritual discipline and growth that she wrote about in her books. Although she was attracted to the Roman Catholic Church she feared restrictions on her intellectual liberty, particularly when the persecution of 'modernists' was unleashed. By 1921 she was reconciled with the Anglican Church. Her first spiritual director, until his death in 1925, was the noted Catholic layman Baron Friedrich von Hugel.

Part of Underhill's ongoing conversion was a growing awareness of social and political issues. She thought of herself as a socialist when she left school, but showed little evidence of this as a young woman. Her response to the First World War was one of jingoistic patriotism (and she worked in an innocuous capacity for Naval Intelligence). However von Hugel encouraged her to move from an interest in mysticism, which focused too much on individual enlightenment, towards a greater understanding of God's self-abasing love made known in history, particularly in Jesus Christ. He stressed too the way in which the church continued that revelation and enabled people to live out its implications in a similar self-giving love here and now. One of the disciplines that Evelyn Underhill undertook in response to von Hugel was a solid round of visiting the slum-dwelling poor of North Kensington. With a typical humorous touch, he had told her: 'I believe you ought to get yourself, gently and gradually, interested *in the poor*; that you should visit them, very quietly and unobtrusively . . . it will, as it were, distribute your blood – some of your blood – away from the brain, where too much of it is lodged at present.'⁵ This discipline opened her eyes to the reality of urban poverty less than a mile away from her comfortable home in fashionable Campden Hill Square.

By the mid 1920s we find an increasing willingness in

Evelyn Underhill to refer to specific social issues, such as poverty, unemployment, slum housing and racial oppression. She did not hesitate to draw attention to these issues in her talks and writings on prayer, and some of her comments must have seemed sharp to her largely middle-class audiences. She was by now convinced that spiritual ideals had to be lived out in action if they were to be a reality. Spirit had to shape the matter of the world. However she never committed herself to any specific social or political programme, and shared the distaste of her class for divisive controversy. Only late in her life did Evelyn Underhill seem to learn that events can lead people to a place where a parting of the ways will occur over specific social or political issues. In her case this came from her commitment to pacifism.

Underhill's teaching on prayer played its own part in bringing the Church of England to a greater awareness of the need for social justice. Her very middle-classness, which is so often a source of criticism today, was also a source of strength. Many of the groups she spoke to were people who shared her privileged background. In such circles prayer tended to be seen as a process of spiritual self-improvement which floated free of engagement with specific social issues. It might be expected to produce greater charity, but not commitment to action. It was precisely this assumption that Underhill increasingly challenged, and often she was speaking to the people who most needed to hear it. More and more she seeks to instil a social conscience in her audiences. For our contemporary tastes it is too understated, and too prone to see the concerned Christian as an individual working for social justice rather than joining with others in groups outside the church. Nevertheless Underhill's spirituality is remarkable for its inclusion of social justice at a time when prayer tended to be divorced from such awareness. Roman Catholic development on such issues had been handicapped earlier in the century by the persecution of modernists (though the Dominican Order kept a lively debate going about the social implications of spirituality). In the Anglican Church priests working in slum areas did their best to make the wider public aware of what was happening to their parishioners, and sometimes used incarnational theology to good effect. But their influence was limited, and spirituality generally still tended to be divorced from pressing social issues. The long haul of changing public attitudes needed all the help it could get. In this situation of the inter-war years it is remarkable that one of the most powerfully persuasive voices was that of a lay woman.

The structure of Underhill's spirituality

A central and crucial element in Evelyn Underhill's spirituality is her belief in God's presence permeating the world: 'There is at every point a penetration by God of the world'.[6] She has an acute sense of the hidden realm of eternity behind and beyond this world. Although hidden, it becomes known through the divine power constantly breaking into this world, to draw it towards the love and perfection that is God's desire for it. Her stress on this permeating divine presence reflects von Hugel's teaching: he himself wrote of 'the penetration of spirit into sense, of the spaceless into space, of the Eternal into time, of God into man'.[7] As part of her thinking on these lines, Evelyn Underhill emphasizes how Spirit bridges the gulf between God and human nature, and makes human nature the place of divine activity. Here she sometimes sounds remarkably like Eckhart, and indeed she was greatly influenced by her reading of him. So it is not surprising to find her writing that 'Our small created spirits originate with God the Pure Spirit, owe their being to Him, and depend utterly on Him.'[8] Because this is a present, ongoing process in which God sustains us in life, in the deepest meaning of that word, we are thus part of the mystery of divine being itself. So (in a yet more Eckhartian mode) she writes that there is 'a certain vital centre of the soul – whether we call it "root", "ground", or "apex" – where God the Uncreated Spirit dwells permanently and substantially'.[9] This is the place 'at which man's centre touches the Absolute . . . is penetrated by the Divine Life'.[10]

It is already worth pausing to begin to draw out the implications of this for a spirituality that seeks to do justice. What Underhill is proposing is a foundational spirituality with a dynamic view of the world. We do not have here a view of the world as a fixed entity, over which human beings struggle to assert themselves. Rather we have a view of the world as constantly bearing within it the divine shaping and loving. And this divine influence is most clearly seen in human beings when they use their freedom to rise above themselves in ways both great and small. Underhill would remind us that Spirit's influence on spirit is not an ethereal, other-worldly concept. Spirit becomes visible in our everyday acts of love, in our endurance when we seek a long-term good, in our loyalty to our ideals, in our determination to seek solutions. Spirit is revealed in that mysterious compulsion we feel to live up to certain standards, or to struggle for justice even when another part of us would gladly settle for a quiet life. In other words, whenever we rise above ourselves in some way, whenever we resist the temptation to put first some narrow calculation of self-interest, we are responding to the gentle pressure of Spirit making itself known in the ground of our being.

I will return to this point later, but want to draw attention to how this leads us to a God who is both transcendent yet a reality *within* us. Here Underhill can sound almost startlingly contemporary. Feminist theologians today sometimes argue that certain images of God can be disabling. Sallie McFague, for example, criticizes monarchical language ('king', 'lord' and so on) on the grounds that it makes us understand God as a monarch both benevolent and severe, loftily dominating the world. In this picture, says McFague, 'God's action is on the world, not in it, and it is a kind of action that inhibits human growth and responsibility.'[11] I am uneasy about this argument, because it seems to me to take insufficient account of how our memory of Jesus alters our understanding of these images. However there is a broader issue of how our knowledge of God can empower us to do God's will in cherishing the earth he created, and working for justice. Evelyn Underhill herself says that a sense of the awesome transcendence of God does not always make us able to respond lovingly. Instead it can bring 'a crushing sense of helplessness; of an unbridged gap between action and contemplation, between the human and the divine'.[12] This is the importance of the understanding of Spirit that she proposes. The God who transcends space and time is the God who is also found in our hearts and minds. Where we see suffering that asks to be alleviated, where we hear the cry of the oppressed and are distressed by it, where we see a broken heart that asks to be mended we are already the place of God's presence and work. Wherever our accustomed horizons are taken away and we see things in a new and more demanding light, it is already God's influence and invitation to be co-workers. God is a reality within us.

Underhill takes over from the seventeenth-century French school of spirituality a threefold pattern of adoration, communion and co-operation as the ideal structure of our prayer life. She believed strongly that each of these three aspects must enter into full prayer, for they enabled a corresponding surrender of mind, heart and will.[13] I will briefly outline her exposition of this pattern, then turn back to consider the implications of Evelyn Underhill's teaching for us today as we seek a spirituality which enables commitment to work for justice and peace.

Her approach to *adoration* is typically bracing. She makes plain that it is not a soupy, wistful state. Rather it is 'the antiseptic of the devotional life, checking those corrupting tendencies to sentimental individualism and sugary effervescence which are always ready to infect it'.[14] This is a shrewd comment. Sentiment, though it may seem to be outward-directed, is always a form of self-indulgence and thus of self-centredness. Adoration, by contrast, draws us away from self-absorption and into that which we adore. The adoration aspect of prayer is thus a means of conquering the natural inclination to put ourselves first, to calculate our self-interest in everything we do (including religion). And, as

Underhill emphasizes, adoration is not a dimension of prayer into which we drop naturally. It grows through our faithfulness to such undramatic disciplines as keeping a daily rule 'without regard to fluctuations in devotional feeling'. It also calls for 'deliberate and repeated acts of attention', and for 'practice of constant brief aspirations towards God'.[15] Adoration then, on the one hand, is a bowing in awe before the divine mystery, which we contemplate like one standing before an infinite sea of love. From this angle adoration is as elevated as one can get. On the other hand adoration is something we grow into through the daily slog of discipline. From this other angle it is a matter of patience, discipline, of the repeated small gesture which we hope will slowly enlarge the capacity of our heart.

Adoration makes possible *communion*, in which we experience the closeness of God. It is an exchange between ourselves and God, who comes to meet us on our own level. In adoration we focus our intellectual awareness on God; in communion we focus our heart. God accepts the love we offer, and draws us into himself. A person experiences a close dependence on God, and God's 'mysterious loving nearness'.[16] Underhill expects experiences of communion to come from within several different aspects of a disciplined prayer life, such as meditation, prayer of simplicity and quiet, and prayer of petition and self-offering. She also stresses that communion, like adoration, is a form of prayer which gradually changes our perspective. To draw close to God is to begin to see the world in a different light. To experience God (for this is what communion is) enhances our awareness of our own shortcomings and those of the world of which we are part. We see the truth about the world and ourselves. And this is no mystical 'intuition'. Rather, Underhill is reminding us that any real experience of God will always show up the contrast between God's loving intentions for the world and the actual state of affairs there. The standards of the kingdom are implanted in us, and because this takes place in the context of knowing God's love, we are at the same time given greater energy and renewed resolve to bring them into the world.

Communion is thus a dynamic experience which moves us to commit ourselves to act out of the love we have experienced. Underhill specifically mentions our powers of discernment, initiative and endurance as being harnessed.[17]

It follows from everything that Evelyn Underhill says about adoration and communion that there need be no contradiction between prayerful absorption into God and commitment to work for justice and peace. On the contrary our devotion to God can be a source of power and commitment for our role in society. This is why she speaks of adoration and communion as being completed by *co-operation*. In particular it completes the movement away from self which develops out of adoration and community. It was a movement which she had known in her own life. Some of her earlier religious involvement had been in some very muddied waters indeed including, around 1905, involvement in an occult group known as the Golden Dawn. This was a short-lived phase, and with her developing interest in mysticism came solider fare. But for a time something remained of her tendency to overstress individual experience (and indeed feelings). Her growth was helped by von Hugel's guidance. In her spiritual journal, Underhill writes on 26 December 1923 that she has felt deeply and clearly the presence of God and of divine love, a love that passes through persons like the water supporting and passing through a shellfish. Then she adds:

> More and more I realize, the union with Christ one craves for can & must be only through union with His redemptive work, always going on in the world. . . So the 'life of supremely happy men' is *not* 'alone with the Alone' – it's the redeeming life, now & in eternity too, in ever greater & more entrancing union with the Spirit of Jesus ceaselessly at *work* in the world.[18]

In her earlier years she had tended to see Jesus as a kind of supreme example of how mystical experience could transform a person. With her reconciliation to the Anglican Church comes her ability to see Jesus as the Son of God inviting us

77

to join other believers in transforming the world in and through him. So her writings on prayer emphasize co-operation as found through participation with others in the Body of Christ. We become an interconnected whole, with an influence permeating the world; we are 'woven into the organism by which the Eternal Spirit acts within the historic scene'.[19] Her teaching on prayer as co-operation has therefore a lively expectation that we will be agents of change.

Co-operation is often seen by her in terms of intercession, but we would be wrong to understand this as simply a form of prayer of petition. By intercession Evelyn Underhill means every intervention we make in the world around us to bring it into conformity with the longing, loving intentions of God. Intercession is thus not limited to overtly religious desires and deeds. It is instead the bringing of all our influence to bear, at whatever level, on the world around us, in the light of our knowledge and love of God. And Underhill repeatedly stresses how, in a sense, we have no choice: all the time we are influencing society around us, shaping its destiny for better or for worse. Growth in prayer can and should give rise to co-operation, in which we use our freedom in ways big and small to draw the world to God's will: 'The protective pity of the intercessor, his willing suffering in and with the souls with which he is charged, the intensity of his detailed care – how close this brings the human spirit to the divine nature; how well this runs in series with the life and mind of Christ.'[20] Co-operation is thus inseparable from our involvement with, indeed our action on the world, in concert with others. Underhill expects a well-formed prayer life to combine the awesomeness of adoration, the uplift of communion, and the costliness of involvement with the pain and need of the world.

The contemporary significance of Evelyn Underhill

Any spirituality which seeks to dispose us towards work for justice and peace must be one which keeps together the vision of God and the reality of this world. Without a growing awareness of God's love and purposes for the world, our ability to give anything to the world is gravely weakened. Without an acute consciousness of the world's pain and distress, our relationship with God is in danger of becoming a self-deceiving flight from reality. I would like to look at each of these aspects in turn, but first we must look at the pressure on us to reduce God to a function of social service.

The temptation to focus on the world at the cost of a relationship with God is one that we constantly face. The intimidating nature of contemporary problems, and the urgency of the need we see, can make it seem as if prayer is a luxury. It is sometimes said, for instance, that our work is our prayer. At other times prayer is seen as good only in so far as it serves some visibly useful purpose. This attitude was one that Underhill had encountered in her own day. She found among young people the insistence that:

> religion is a social activity, and service is its proper expression: that all valid knowledge of God is social, and He is chiefly known in mankind: that the use of prayer is mainly social, in that it improves us for service, otherwise it must be condemned as a merely selfish activity.[21]

Elsewhere she comments that many devoted Christians believe that the best thing is to keep busy, giving themselves 'no time to take what is offered to those who abide quietly with Christ; because there seem such a lot of urgent jobs. . . The result of this can only be a maiming of their human nature, exhaustion, loss of depth and of vision.'[22] Of course, she stresses, the spiritual values we know through God must be lived out in committed service in the world around us. But, she adds, unless we take time to know and love God for his own sake then we will have nothing to offer the world except our own rampant egos, and 'neither our judgments upon the social order nor our active social service will be perfectly performed'.[23]

This is, I think, a shrewd judgment and one that we need

to hear today. It is backed up by her entire teaching on prayer: her vision of that other realm of God, constantly breaking into and bearing upon this one, and her threefold system of adoration, communion and co-operation, which certainly takes action seriously, but sees it in the context of our knowledge and love of God. Now it might be objected that this is a long way from the spirit of our times, and from liberation theology in particular. Not necessarily. Consider this passage from Gustavo Gutierrez's *A Theology of Liberation*, sometimes credited as having been *the* work which sparked off worldwide interest in liberation theology:

> the knowledge that at the root of our personal and community existence lies the gift of the self-communication of God, the grace of his friendship, fills our life with gratitude. It allows us to see our encounters with men, our loves, everything that happens in our life as a gift. There is real love only when there is free giving – without conditions or coercion. Only gratuitous love goes to our very roots and elicits true love.
>
> Prayer is an experience of gratuitousness. This 'leisure' action, this 'wasted' time, reminds us that the Lord is beyond the categories of useful and useless.[24]

Prayer, he is reminding us, is not primarily a means of self-improvement or even of world-improvement. It is a relationship which grows out of the knowledge of God's love for us, and brings freedom precisely because it depends on our uncompelled responsiveness. God shows his love, then waits on us to respond or otherwise.

We are not important for God because of our success, or achievements, or usefulness. We are loved by God simply because . . . we are loved by God. The more we can integrate this simple truth, the more we discover our self-worth. This truth creates a freedom in us to act committedly for social change, because we have nothing to prove by it. We do not have to earn our standing with God. It is always freely on offer. And, as Gutierrez points out, we begin to see how our deepest relationships reflect the same freely-given love.

I would suggest then, that a spirituality of justice and peace begins with the fact of God's love for us, and for each person in the world. By drawing us into this awareness it frees us to act out of the security and worth that we receive through that love. This ties in with what we learned from Eckhart in Chapter 3 about not making other people components of our plans, and thus extensions of our egos. It ties in too with Merton's critique of instrumentalism to be discussed in Chapter 5. (Instrumentalism in the sense of the tendency to view people – and nature – as significant only in terms of their usefulness.)

A spirituality for social change should thus recognize that all that we do or seek is founded on our knowledge of God's prior, unconditional love for us. This is our security. However we should not expect it to be a source of serenity. One of the fruits of our journey into God is a steady movement away from self-centredness. Underhill speaks of this as 'growth and movement from the individual to the universal standpoint'.[25] In this she is surely correct: movement into God is a movement into reality, into the truth of things. One reason why this is so is the fact that spiritual growth enlarges our capacity to love. Movement into God is a movement away from self-absorption. Long-term love begins to overtake our immediate desires and enable 'a complete transformation of the self's centre of interest'.[26] Underhill also speaks of this as a 'universalizing' of our will and love.[27]

This is where it is important to remain in touch with the reality of the world's suffering. If our love is to reflect God's love and our will God's will, then we must be as aware as possible of the reality of life in our world. Without such an awareness we will not be able to co-operate with the divine purpose; and co-operation, Underhill has reminded us, is an essential element of prayer. Indeed she insists that to be a Christian is to expect to be an agent of change: if we ask God to do something about 'the social and economic miseries which our Christian civilization has produced', then we should be prepared to follow the prayer with an Ignatian act of consecration: 'Take Lord and receive, all *my* liberty, *my* memory, *my* understanding, *my* will, all *I* have and possess.'[28] She insists that prayer implies a preparedness to do all we can physically, mentally and spiritually to change the face of the earth. This insistence links, of course, with her teaching on co-operation as an essential element of prayer.

It has often been said that prayer requires our active preparedness to act on what we have prayed about. However one element that is necessary for such action is our insight, our alert awareness about the needs of the times. Underhill's emphasis on the consecration of our mental faculties underscores this point. Since she wrote, the world's increased complexity and interdependence has increased the need for praying, concerned Christians to be alert and well-informed. Without these qualities the action that arises out of their prayer will be much less effective. Often enough there is no lack of goodwill and concern among Christians. What tends to be lacking is a preparedness to analyse, to interpret, to seek not only to know the news but to discern what lies behind it. To look on the surface of events is not enough. Jesus himself said that those who could not see the significance of what he was doing were people who looked without seeing, listened without hearing or understanding. And, he added, this dull inertia came from a combination of hardness of heart and fear of the challenge of change, that had grown over the years (Mt. 13:13–15). They were unable to read the signs of the times (Mt. 16:1–3).

Throughout I have been suggesting that a spirituality of justice and peace is one that requires a 'spark in the soul' – a movement of love in our heart which responds to God's love by committing us to love the world which is the creation of his love. From Evelyn Underhill we learn that the spark in the soul demands co-operation with God. Co-operation, however, presupposes an informed alertness, an awareness of what is going on in our world and of the forces shaping it and us. If we do not learn such discernment we will, in effect, be abdicating responsibility for the world. Unless we are

aware of the genesis and causes of events we will be unable
to do anything about them in any lasting sense. Without a
concerned, well-informed alertness, we treat social and economic developments as unexpected and unpredictable events.
If we do not attempt to enlarge our understanding of our
world, and pause from time to time to analyse it, then its
developments will seem to come from nowhere, without
reason and beyond explanation. But prayer – as Underhill
reminds us – is an assumption of responsibility for the world.
In true prayer there is preparedness to co-operate with God,
who is always seeking to draw the world towards his perfection. Prayer implies co-operation, and co-operation
demands an aware alertness about what is going on in the
world. In other words, if we take Underhill's approach
seriously, we will not be content with surface realities. We
will want to know what is going on underneath.

When it comes to political and social issues we find ourselves in a realm of sometimes bewildering claim and counter-
claim, in which it is not always easy to see beyond surface
appearances. Probably the best way in is to ask the question,
'Who profits?' Many alleged social reforms turn out, when
that question is asked, to be disguised ways of serving the
interests of the more powerful sections of society. However
for many people even this line of questioning may seem difficult and too analytical. So how can we deepen our understanding of the developments taking place in society, the
better to co-operate with the work of God? Fortunately we
are not called upon to become experts in economics, politics
or sociology. There are some simple steps open to all of us
which can increase our understanding of the world, and our
ability to co-operate with God in caring for it. In fact even
'experts' in contemporary affairs might benefit from these
steps, since there is an understanding through the heart which
is just as necessary as understanding through the head.

The first step is to become conscious of how our beliefs
about social and political issues are formed. All the time we
are being influenced. It is surprising how little we stop to
reflect on who or what is influencing us. So when working

with groups on a spirituality for social justice, I sometimes ask participants to take a few minutes to compile on a sheet of paper their individual answers to the question, 'Who or what influences my social/political thinking today?' The answers often begin with the media, such as television news and newspaper reports. Other common sources include, as might be expected, conversations with friends and family. (Sometimes people report conversations with their parents as influential, in so far as they reacted *against* their parents' view.) For some people exposure to the Bible has been crucial, especially the prophets and the gospels. Pop music is sometimes cited by younger people. Few people cite soap operas, though these too can form people's images of society. When did you see a poor or handicapped person in *Dynasty* or *Dallas*? People pondering the question more deeply sometimes conclude, to their surprise, that they cannot always answer it, to the extent that some of their social and political views 'have always been there' – and sometimes these are little more than prejudices. The answer to the question may produce then, a variety of influences, some of them helping us discover the truth about the world, some of them concealing it. We become more conscious of the variety of influences on us, and by so doing become more able to control them.

The second step is to become aware of the voices of the victims of the world: the poor, the oppressed and those who find themselves treated as the discards of society. We ought to become aware too of creation's voice as it cries out with pain at our despoliation of the environment. Do we hear these voices? And do they accordingly influence our social and political views? The inner truth about society can be more accurately revealed by these testimonies than by any number of statistics or theories. This points back to Chapter 2, in which I refer to the importance of compassion, of seeing through the eyes of others, and of the role that 'praying the news' can play in this. The alertness and insight that our spirituality must contain does not depend on great gifts of intellectual analysis. On the contrary we are pointed back to the spark in the soul – to the warmth and responsiveness of our hearts. True insight and alertness grow from our ability to listen to the voices of the world. Evelyn Underhill expected people who were faithful in prayer to be working for change. Furthering the purposes of God, she noted, required in turn 'a direct responsibility as regards our whole use of created things: money, time, position, the politics we support, the papers we read.'[29] This list itself underlines the importance of awareness, of seeing the truth about the world.

Some liberation theologians speak of the poor as 'epistemologically privileged', meaning that they have a better view of reality. Their exposure to the sharp end of life gives them first-hand knowledge of the truth. When do we listen to them, and how does what they say influence us? If we put their testimonies side by side with the sources that usually influence us, then we have a useful yardstick with which to gauge our perceptions of the world. If the voices of the poor and marginalized do not influence us, then we have to ask searching questions about our sources of information. People watching television news (for example) usually do not realize the enormous effort made by governments and corporations to get their point of view across. Government departments employ teams of press officers to put their ministers, and their ministers' views, in the forefront of the public consciousness. (Arranging photo or film opportunities for them has been elevated to an art.) Big companies or institutions similarly employ public relations officers to project a favourable image of themselves. Inevitably editors tend to use this wealth of information and pictures put at their disposal when compiling news programmes.

The same media bring us news of the poor much less frequently; the outlook of the poor is hardly reflected at all. Who are the poor? They can be the victims of torture in South Africa, or the homeless young people hustling on the local streets. They can be prisoners awaiting execution in the United States, or the handicapped person living next door. However, if our spirituality is to be *real*, from time to time we need to ask whether we are hearing the voices of those on the margins of society who are literally our neighbours. The

Brazilian theologian Clodovis Boff had this to say to the people of Europe:

> You will excuse me if I am blunt, but you Europeans seem to me dominated by an uncontrollable unconscious urge to turn all problems, even the starkest, into mere 'cultural facts', topics for conversation, articles and inconclusive debates. You possess a vast culture, but it is a dematerialized culture, disconnected from life and apart from history.[30]

He is referring, I think, to the way we view the actual poverty and injustice that we see in our own society. It tends to be seen as created by forces beyond our control. Even those of us whose consciences are disturbed by poverty tend not to think of the poor or victims of injustice as part of *our* story, as connected with *our* shared history. History, in fact, has been relegated to theme parks, or has become a 'heritage industry'. History is not a narrative about how society rewards some citizens at the expense of others. Listening to the victims of society has the advantage of helping us to focus on concrete realities here and now, the kind of realities which need to be transformed if a different world is to be created. Clodovis Boff says that this is why the church in Europe *needs* the poor for its own future:

> To me it seems as clear as day that there is no future for the church except at the side of those who do not have the present, but only the future – the oppressed! Church movements made up mainly of the non-poor, decision-makers, liberal professionals and students, may lay claim to an improved present, but not to a different future.[31]

Underhill took seriously the need for a society to learn from its treatment of the poor. She believed that 'corporate regeneration' of society required its citizens to look honestly into 'the true springs' of its conduct. This would involve discovering 'the humiliating facts about those impulses which really condition our behaviour in such matters as nationalism, property, employment, servitude, sex'. And then:

> Having reached the level of self-knowledge, it may perhaps be brought to something equivalent to social penitence: may feel as a direct reproach every life damaged by bad housing, every child maimed by economic conditions, every soul stifled by luxury or obsessed by unreal values, every man and woman embittered and made hopeless by unemployment and friendlessness.[32]

If we train ourselves to listen to the voices coming from the heart of the world, we find that it is more than a message of pain and loss. It is also, often enough, a message of hope, endurance and faith. This is why liberation theologians suggest that we can be evangelized by the poor. In so many cases suffering does not crush them, nor does oppression make them give up hope. They endure, strengthened by faith and by the conviction that a better future is still possible. Listening to the voices of the poor reveals the truth about society, and over a period will help us form priorities for action. But the same voices can also encourage and inspire us. Here is one example of that courage we sometimes find among the poor or those who suffer for justice. Mirna Anaya is a lawyer in El Salvador who worked for eight years defending political prisoners there. Her husband Herbert was director of the El Salvador Committee for Human Rights. On 26 October 1988 he was shot dead as he was driving two of his children to school. He had been previously imprisoned and tortured, and had received many death threats – like Archbishop Romero before him. His death left Mirna and their children devastated. Yet she was able to say:

> Herbert was a man of great faith and the people placed their faith in him too. . . Barefoot peasants who had walked for miles pressed pennies into my hand, knowing how hard it was going to be for me and my five children. . . Before, I had but one home; now, all doors are open to me. I

had only one family; now, people welcome me everywhere. (*Tablet*, 10 December 1988)

Meditation on experiences such as this can help us deepen our acceptance of responsibility within society, and find solidarity with the poor. With regard to honest awareness of the truth of our society, I can cite a meditation by Underhill herself. In a talk given to a conference at Swanwick in 1922 she develops a meditation by evoking the beauties of spring in the English countryside, 'snowy with hawthorn, the downs starred with tiny perfect flowers, the amazing emerald life of the young beechwoods, the exultant singing of the birds'. She then invites us to hear God saying to us, 'Behold and see! This is my creation!' Then she says:

> But now, reverse this picture; and suppose that we are condemned to go with Christ to some of the places which we, in our corporate capacity – Christian citizens of a Christian country – have made, or allowed through stupidity and sloth to come into existence. Imagine any one of us walking through the East End of London . . . or down our prison corridors – or through a poison-gas factory – with that Companion at our side. And suppose that it is our turn to meet that glance and say, 'Behold and see! This is *our* creation!'[33]

This is a powerful meditation, partly because of the way our expectations are shaped by a lyrically pastoral beginning, only to be led – as with parables – into an unexpected conclusion. It drives home the contrast between God's love and goodness on the one hand, and the exploitation and destructive evil at work among us on the other. Yet the response should take us beyond guilt, to motivation, because we venture into the human darkness with Christ at our side.

I also mentioned meditation as useful in developing a sense of solidarity with the poor and marginalized. Sometimes this is possible in actual Eucharists that I attend in inner London, where so many of my fellow-worshippers are black or elderly or gay or migrant workers. Their faces are faces of strength, dignity and triumph over adversity. Sometimes it is possible to meditate further afield in the Eucharist. Celebration of the Eucharist takes place in widely different settings and cultures. Surely there is not a moment when the Eucharist is not being celebrated somewhere on earth? And so I think sometimes about where else it could be being celebrated: in a black township of South Africa, on the death row of a United States prison, in complete secrecy in Albania by people who risk their lives for it. The Eucharist draws all of us into the same presence of God, celebrates God's re-creation of the earth while commemorating Jesus' sacrificial death for us.

I also find that the presence of Jesus in the Blessed Sacrament can lead to a rich meditation along the same lines. In silence we find ourselves before a tabernacle or aumbry, where the warm glow of a candle tells us that we come into the Lord's presence here. But – and it is a great mystery – there is not one presence in London, another in Rio de Janeiro, yet another in Bombay. There is one Jesus, present to us always in loving silence, to whom we come with our prayers and adoration. And so I like to think that every time we come before the Blessed Sacrament we come not just into the presence of the Lord, but into the presence of all those other people who gather round the tabernacle all over the world. Who is that whispering her prayers on the other side? Is it a native Indian woman in Peru, telling Jesus in Quechua that her baby is dying of starvation? And what is that old black man saying? Is he asking Jesus to protect his teenage grandson from torture in prison in South Africa? This is creative imagination, of course. Yet I think it draws me into the reality of the world as it lies before God, a reality that is too often at variance with his own love, and which challenges me to play whatever part I can in his redemptive work.

Earlier in this chapter I mentioned how Underhill shares with Eckhart a strong sense of God within. The Spirit of God works within human spirits, stirring up our consciences, not allowing us to be satisfied with the way things are. The perseverance of the poor and oppressed, their refusal to accept the status quo, their rejection of the blame for their own poverty, their conviction that things can be changed – in these and other ways there is evidence of God at work in them. We can take heart from this, just as we can take heart from evidence of God at work in us too. If we are disturbed by the plight of the poor, if we are angry at the exploitation of the powerless, if we are distressed by the visible plight of the marginalized in our own society, then *already* we know the power of God. A spirituality of justice and peace is not obedience to exterior laws and precepts; it is a responsiveness to God making himself known within us as he opens our eyes to the world around us, and helps us to listen to the voices coming from within its depths. This should help us avoid the exhaustion and burnout that can come from our awareness of the needs of the world. God is already within us, helping us see them and discern the challenge they pose. The question then becomes how, and where, we can co-operate with God's work. Prayer is indispensable when it comes to answering this question, which should lead us to concentrate our energies and accept that what we can do will always be limited.

Nevertheless everyone needs to have some area in which they are working for justice and peace, seeking to co-operate with God in changing how things are in the world. To believe in God is to believe that things cannot be left as they are. To move deeper into prayer is to move deeper into our responsiveness to God's love; the spark in our soul flares more brightly. Prayer, as Underhill notes, implies that we are seeking an ever greater awareness of God's work in the world, and are therefore in the forefront of seeking change:

Those who cling to tradition and fear all novelty in God's relation with His world deny the creative activity of the Holy Spirit, and forget that what is now tradition was once innovation; that the real Christian is always a revolutionary, belongs to a new race, and has been given a new name and a new song. God is with the future.[34]

Over the years we can observe Evelyn Underhill practising

what she preached. As noted earlier, she shrank from political involvement in the narrow sense, because of her dislike of divisiveness and because she wanted to reach as many people as possible.[35] Yet there are clear intimations of a developing social conscience. During the First World War she had been the author of poems and articles which were strongly and conventionally patriotic. In 1915 she was capable of writing that war brought good as well as evil, and that for people with faith 'the particular form or moment in which death comes . . . surely cannot matter very much'.[36] Seven years later her stance is very different. Faith and prayer have deepened her, have helped her listen to the world and see where change is needed. In a speech in 1922 she condemned acquisitiveness, blind support of one's own class or country, combative games and destructive sports as reversion to a half-savage state of mind.[37] Her pilgrimage of faith has by this point led her out from the preconceptions, prejudices and stereotyped way of thinking of her class. This is not the voice of a typical prosperous lawyer's wife, nor does it contain any of the frivolity which seized so many middle-class people in England in the early 1920s before recession struck. It is the voice of one who has struggled to read the signs of the times.

She maintained this prophetic stance, retaining her pacifism through the war years until her death in 1941. She was a member of the Peace Pledge Union and the Anglican Pacifist Fellowship. During the Second World War she was well aware of the evil represented by Nazism, and at one point wrote to her friend Mildred Bosanquet: 'The nation as a whole obviously feels it right to fight this war out, and must I think do so.'[38] But one of the reasons she maintained her pacifism was her concern that some people should be able to witness to the truth that war was never in itself an adequate answer to anything. Thus she wrote to another correspondent, Fr Geoffrey Curtis, CR, saying that she was 'more and more convinced that the idea that this or any other war is "righteous" or will achieve any creative result of a durable kind, is an illusion.'[39] She was particularly concerned that God should not be invoked to bless war, even the war-making of the Allies. In a letter published in *Time and Tide* in 1940 she wrote:

> though many Christians find themselves driven to the use of force in the present crisis, they may feel chary of invoking religious sanctions for their military acts. In view of our past record can any of us dare to say that a victory of our arms would necessarily be a victory for the Spirit of God?[40]

Her loathing of war came from her ability to hear the broken victims rather than the triumphant speeches. Strong discipline in prayer and Christian orthodoxy had brought her to a place where she was able to go beyond the easy clichés and well-worn assumptions of many people around her, and reach for a deeper truth as inspiration for herself and whoever would listen to her. Her spirituality had worked. The spark in her soul, her responsive love to God and openness to the world, had helped her move towards a universal viewpoint transcending her own self-interest and that of her class. This same responsive love had made her acutely conscious of the disparity between the pain of the world, and God's loving will for it. From this awareness had come her desire to co-operate with God, and as part of her co-operation to listen more attentively to the world. Evelyn Underhill's spirituality gives us the courage to believe that what we do *can* make a difference. As she herself says, 'It is our business to prepare, so far as we may, a favourable atmosphere and environment for the children who will make the future: and this environment is not anything mysterious, it is simply ourselves.'[41]

1   Janet Grierson, *The Deaconess* (London, 1981), p. 24. Although she supported the work of deaconesses, Underhill did not believe in the ordination of women to the priesthood. See her comments in *Mixed Pasture* (London, 1933), p. 113. Nevertheless her writing has begun to attract the attention of writers tracing the work of pioneering women. See Dana Greene, 'Toward an evaluation of the thought of Evelyn Underhill', *History of European Ideas*, vol. 8, no. 4/5 (1987).
2   Grierson, pp. 62, 68.

3 For the controversy over the 1916 mission, see ibid., pp. 43–4; also Brian Heeney, *The Women's Movement in the Church of England 1850–1930* (Oxford, 1988), pp. 121–2. For the comments of Dean Henry Wace and the report of Dr Fairfield, see ibid., pp. 124–5.

4 Quoted in Christopher Armstrong, *Evelyn Underhill: an introduction to her life and writings* (Oxford, 1975), pp. 65, 67. For her atheism, see ibid., p. 31.

5 Quoted in Margaret Cropper, *Evelyn Underhill* (London, 1958), p. 75.

6 Evelyn Underhill, *Mixed Pasture*, p. 98.

7 Quoted in Evelyn Underhill, *The Golden Sequence* (London, 1932), p. 25.

8 *The Golden Sequence*, p. 24.

9 ibid., p. 54.

10 Evelyn Underhill, *Mysticism*, 12th edn (London, 1960), p. 55.

11 Sallie McFague, *Models of God* (London, 1987), p. 68.

12 *The Golden Sequence*, p. viii.

13 ibid., p. 175. In her earlier writing, however, Underhill retains the older threefold scheme of purgation, illumination and union.

14 Evelyn Underhill, *Man and the Supernatural* (London, 1927), p. 214.

15 ibid., p. 207.

16 ibid., p. 216.

17 ibid., p. 218.

18 Quoted in Armstrong, op. cit., pp. 222–3.

19 *Man and the Supernatural*, p. 234.

20 ibid., p. 264.

21 *The Life of the Spirit and the Life of Today* (London, 1922), pp. 206–7.

22 *Mixed Pasture*, p. 75.

23 *The Life of the Spirit and the Life of Today*, p. 208.

24 Gustavo Gutierrez, *A Theology of Liberation* (London, 1974), p. 206.

25 *Man and the Supernatural*, p. 218.

26 ibid., p. 224.

27 ibid., p. 233.

28 *Mixed Pasture*, p. 102.

29 Evelyn Underhill, *Abba* (London, 1956), p. 33.

30 Clodovis Boff, *The Way Forward for the First World Church*, CIIR, Third World Theology ser. (London, 1986), p. 8.

31 ibid., p. 10.

32 *Mixed Pasture*, pp. 81–2.

33 ibid., pp. 66–7.

34 *Abba*, p. 34.

35 Armstrong, op. cit., pp. 242–3.

36 Quoted in Robert G. Woods, 'The future we shan't see: Evelyn Underhill's pacificism', *The Christian Century* (16 May 1979), p. 554.

37 *Mixed Pasture*, pp. 80–1.

38 Charles Williams (ed.), *The Letters of Evelyn Underhill* (London, 1944), p. 308.

39 ibid., p. 268.
40 Quoted in Margaret Cropper, op. cit., p. 228.
41 *The Life of the Spirit and the Life of Today*, p. 216.

5

Thomas Merton and God Our Identity

Thomas Merton (1915–1968) is probably the most famous monk of the twentieth century. His renown began when his autobiography, *The Seven Storey Mountain*, was published in 1948. It describes how he found God and became a monk after a lonely, wandering existence in which he had flirted with communism and led an occasionally dissolute life. Somehow his life story seemed to catch the bitter-sweet, searching mood of the post-war period, when many people adjusting to ordinary life after years of war found themselves seeking a source of meaning. Merton's account of his own quest quickly sold 600,000 copies before going into paperback.[1]

The book was a success because it seemed to resonate in the lives of those who read it. Merton had the uncanny knack of writing in a way which made many others feel that he was saying what they were thinking. It was a gift that continued in the dozens of books and hundreds of articles that he wrote in the succeeding twenty years. Always a prolific writer, even he found it difficult to keep up with the requests for articles; at one point he wrote testily in his journal that editors seemed to think that he secreted articles like perspiration.[2]

From 1941 onwards he lived in the Cistercian abbey of Our Lady of Gethsemani in Kentucky, and indeed for his last few years was in a hermitage there. Through the years Merton's writing changed direction and focus. Moving deeper into prayer and solitude seemed to sharpen his awareness of what was going on in the world. He thought, prayed and wrote about many of the most pressing issues of our time: racism, poverty, war, and western society's loss of direction. But he was an acute observer and penetrating judge of social developments. Once again his writings resonated in people's lives. Many of those who shared his pain at the oppression and injustice of the world felt that he wrote for them. His books have been translated into twenty-three languages.[3]

The course of Merton's life illustrates many of the paradoxes of contemplative spirituality. Here we have a person who became a Cistercian monk in order to find God in seclusion and silence, hidden from the world. But, as Merton discovered, it is impossible to draw closer to God without drawing closer to the world again, loving it and holding it before God in prayer. But Merton was exceptional in his well-informed and penetrating understanding of what was going on in society. His love of God and world is a superb example of the spark in the soul. God loves his creation, and those who would love God learn to look on the world with God's own eyes of love. Merton loved the world and linked himself with its pain and grief through his prayer and writing. We will return to those points later in the chapter when we discuss Merton's teaching on contemplative prayer.

As part of his withdrawal from the world, Merton was vowed to a life of silence. Yet his books and articles spoke loudly and eloquently. His prophetic witness won him many friends – and some enemies. It helped create a correspondence that is staggering both in volume and diversity. His correspondents included Dorothy Day, Boris Pasternak, the Dalai Lama, Martin Luther King, Ernesto Cardenal, D. T. Suzuki (Zen master), Abdul Aziz (Sufi mystic), Rabbi Abraham Heschel, Daniel Berrigan, Rosemary Ruether, and Jacques Maritain. In the Merton archives at Bellarmine College, Louisville, Kentucky, there are over 1800 folders of correspondence, some of them containing as many as 200 letters.[4] It is ironic that a few years after entering the monastery Merton wrote in his journal, 'By the grace of God it was easy for me to forget the world as soon as I left it. I never wanted to go back.'[5] However the frequent clatter of Merton's typewriter was to show that despite these earlier protestations, the world was very much in his thoughts. This tension between his desire for an integrating silence and his need to relate to people was to permeate his life as a monk.[6]

There was another tension in his life. Like all of us, Merton was a spiritual person and a sensual one. Like many of us, he knew a lifelong struggle to integrate the two. During his time as an undergraduate at Cambridge he had fathered an illegitimate child. Much later in life, after more than twenty years in vows, he fell deeply in love with a nurse who cared for him during a spell in hospital. He dissembled to other monks and broke many monastic rules in order to continue meeting her afterwards. His abbot found out about the relationship and asked Merton to choose between her and his commitment to the monastic life. Merton chose the latter. He felt torn apart and devastated by having to choose in this way. But out of this conflict came healing. The man who had many times felt unlovable now knew himself to have been deeply loved, and never despaired in that way again.[7]

Merton's personal paradoxes are linked with what he has to tell us today through his teaching on spirituality. The English words wholeness and holiness share the same Anglo-Saxon root. This should not surprise us. The God who is true holiness asks us to bring the whole of ourselves to him; he also binds together our fragmented, divided identities through his love, acceptance and forgiveness of us. Merton sought holiness and wholeness, a oneness with God in which the divergent aspects of his character would be transformed and knit together. He began by trying to deny the writer and the sensual man much concerned about the world. He ended by finding that God could use the whole of him.

If we bear Merton's paradoxes in mind we will not be surprised to find that the question of identity is a frequently recurring theme in Merton's writings. He stresses repeatedly that our true self is frequently unknown, even to ourselves, and is to be discovered only in and through God. Identity will therefore be the first aspect of Merton's teaching I will outline in this chapter. The second theme of Merton I will look at is his emphasis on the importance of solitude and silence. Solitude and silence can help us see through the distortions that are current in society, and to discern the truth. And to see the truth is a precondition for discovering new possibilities in society, as we have been reminded by Evelyn Underhill in Chapter 4. Thirdly I want to examine what Merton has to say about contemplative consciousness. I believe that here he helps us recover a wholeness of vision that has many repercussions, ranging from how we see our 'enemy' to how we treat nature.

Finding our identity

Merton was always deeply sceptical about understanding our identity in terms of being well-adjusted to society, of having achieved something. He wrote:

> We are all too ready to believe that the self we have created out of our more or less inauthentic efforts ... is a 'real self'. We even take it for our identity ... [But] our real person ... is hidden in mystery. Who will you find that has enough faith and self-respect to attend to this mystery and begin by accepting himself as *unknown*? God help the man who thinks he knows all about himself.[8]

What will it mean for us if we take Merton's advice and have the 'faith and self-respect' to view our identities as unknown? Deep within us lurks the belief that we make ourselves. This is probably a more common phenomenon in the outwardly confident and prosperous nations of the northern hemisphere. Here we find stress on self-achievement, on a strong individualism. With his usual gift for a biting phrase, Merton refers to the 'elephantiasis of self-will' found in western society, and adds for good measure that it also produced 'inordinate self-consciousness ... monumental self-awareness ... obsession with self-affirmation'.[9] Merton links this egocentricity with the uncritical approach to human power which allows science and technology to operate unconstrained by human values – a point we will take up later in the chapter.

Why is Merton so critical of the general belief that people make themselves, forge their own identities out of their strength? I think he is warning us that those who believe they are autonomous beings with unlimited possibilities discover, on the contrary, that they have imprisoned themselves. The emphasis on self-sufficiency eats away at people's ability to relate to others; the emphasis on self-awareness makes it difficult for them to leave self behind sufficiently to enter and explore other ideals and alternative visions. A society develops in which individuals are locked into furthering their own interests, and disregard the human growth that can only come from a shared vision of the common good.

Merton reminds us what we really seek and need are 'love, an authentic identity, a life that has meaning'. No amount of willing can bring them within reach, he says, for they:

> come to us only as gifts, and in order to receive them as gifts we have to be open. In order to be open we have to renounce ourselves, in a sense we have to *die* to our image of ourselves, our autonomy, our fixation on our self-willed identity.[10]

This is a hard lesson to learn, and just as hard for those who are active in campaigning on justice and peace issues. Our spontaneous answer might be to deny this. After all, if we are active in work for social change we are usually aware of battling against the status quo, and of striving to resist the momentum of a technological, materialist society that seems to be out of control. Surely it is the personnel of the military–industrial complex who typify the attitude described by Merton, namely belief in limitless human power?

Certainly Merton reserved some of his choicest invective for technology run amok. He regarded today's central problem as the uncritical attitude shown towards the technological mind: 'No matter how monstrous, no matter how criminal an act may be, if it is justified by science it is unassailable.'[11] And yet I wonder if it is right for those of us who work for social change to evade Merton's strictures. It smacks a little too much of 'I thank you, God, that I am not grasping, unjust, adulterous like the rest of mankind' (Lk 18:11). The truth is that in the sometimes frustrating and occasionally lonely struggle for justice and peace we can fall into the trap of self-justifying autonomy. It can all too easily seem as if everything depends on our efforts. Down this road lie potential violence ('we must *do* something') or despair ('it's no use'). It is something of a shock to discover that Merton, whom we could almost call the patron saint of war-resisters, was deeply sceptical of aspects of the peace movement of his day, whose consciousness he described as 'activistic'.[12] And in words which ought to be engraved on every peace activist's heart he wrote:

> To allow oneself to be carried away by a multitude of conflicting concerns, to surrender oneself to too many demands, to commit oneself to too many projects, to want to help everyone in everything is to succumb to violence. More than that, it is co-operation in violence. The frenzy of the activist neutralizes his work for peace. It destroys his own inner capacity for peace. It destroys the fruitfulness of his own work, because it kills the root of inner wisdom which makes the work fruitful.[13]

Merton's warning here is that sometimes those who work for justice and peace can reflect the assertiveness and even ruthlessness of those whom they seek to resist. Let me give an example. The religious order to which I belong has a house in the Plaistow area of East London. The Tube train on the way there passes one piece of graffito painted on a wall in letters several feet high. It shouts: 'Smash racism! Smash fascism!' The violence of the language of smashing sows doubts in my mind about what is being offered. It is a short step from smashing racism and fascism to smashing the skulls of racists and fascists. Perhaps this is initially an attractive prospect, but it is one which leaves us different from the racists and fascists in degree only. It was this implicit violence, and the accompanying sectarianism, that did much to discredit the Left in Britain in the 1970s.

Merton points us back to the question of what it is that we act out *of*. When we resist oppression, struggle for justice or witness for peace, what is the source of our actions? In the metaphor I am using in this book, it should be the spark in the soul, where the divine life imparts something of itself to each person, and where we find ourselves loving the world which God loves. In each of us there is this unknown area where we are called into being through our direct relationship with God, as we saw with Eckhart. Merton, like Eckhart, believes that each person has an unknown ground of being.[14] Our desires to work for justice and peace, to end human suffering and in particular to banish the clouds of war, come from this deep centre of our being. We know this because such desires are not comfortable to live with. They are desires that assert themselves within us, to the extent of making us prepared to stand out, quite literally: by vigilling, protest marching, leafleting, writing to people in power. We sometimes wish that this prompting would leave us alone and allow us to sink into comfortable anonymity. Yet although these desires come from our depths, we should not confuse them with our identity as such.

Just as those who worship technology can get trapped in it, so too we who work for justice and peace can become impoverished if we rely solely on our ideals. Certainly these give us enthusiasm, vision and drive. But in the long run ideals are not enough. Action can burn us out and compassion can drain us. We need to be sustained, even in our ideals, by that hidden ground of our being where we know God. It is God who, through making us in God's own image (Gen. 1:26), gives us the very power to love and to dream of what could be for the world. So even when we are returning God's love, it is in a sense God at work in us. This is why Merton speaks of our identity as unknown: our identity is something which ultimately opens up into the infinity of God. We are who we are not because of a list of personality attributes, a compendium of ideals, or a range of activity. Rather we are who we are because of God's imparting of the power of love. Or as Merton puts it, 'Here the individual is aware of himself as a self-to-be-dissolved in self-giving, in love, in "letting-go", in ecstasy, in God.'[15] Hence the paradox that we are most who we are when we let go of who we are. If we find our importance or our security, or our sense of worth in being a tireless campaigner or a recognized social critic, we are in dangerous territory. By contrast the more a person finds his or her identity through knowing God in love, the more, in the long run, that person will be able to do for social justice.

This does not diminish the need to work for justice and peace, nor the urgency of the task facing us. But it does remind us that personal spirituality is inseparable from the work for social change. Sometimes in the Christian justice and peace movement the prevailing ethos can seem to be one of action, of strong resolve, of a highly articulate, high profile determination. There can sometimes be a disparagement of stillness, of conversion and the means of grace.

We have to take time to open ourselves to the nourishing love of God which gives us our identity. It means making space for the sacraments. It means allowing for stillness and silence. It means trying to find a balance and reciprocity between committed action and reposing in God. These things allow the spark in the soul whereby we move deeper into God and deeper into our caring love for the world. We create in ourselves an inner disposition out of which we can act freely, and a strength which can see us through many difficult situations. I knew and greatly admired a church minister in South Africa who regularly went on retreat in the barren Karoo semi-desert, with just his Bible and a water bottle. He was a tireless anti-apartheid campaigner, and one day was arrested by the security police. In their interrogation they asked him why he associated with uncivilized people – meaning blacks.

He told me: 'I asked the police what made them think *they* were civilized. Then they picked me up and threw me against a wall.'

'What happened then?' I asked.

102

He replied: 'When I got my breath back, I told them, "See what I mean?" '

To take time off to nourish our relationship with God helps us to discover our identity afresh, in terms of gift from God. What is bestowed is not a one-off identity, a character that we can slip into like a hand into a glove. Instead we are given the security of constant love and the assurance of absolute worth – and the knowledge that these are ours unearned. 'As faith deepens', says Merton, 'and as communion deepens with it, it becomes more and more intensive and at the same time reaches out to affect everything else we think and do.'[16] The best resource for commitment to social action is to grow in awareness of this gratuitous love, which in turn enables the spark in our soul, through which we love God and the creation which God loves.

Silence and solitude

When the people of Judah looked at themselves from the perspective of the exile, they sometimes felt that the future held little but despair. Their prophets were unable to give any vision from the Lord (Lam. 2:9), and no one knew how long the situation would last (Ps. 74:9). They were a people without hope for the future.

Prophecy and hope have always been closely linked. Prophecy in the Judaeo–Christian tradition is more than a crude foretelling of what will transpire in the future. Prophecy is a person's ability to pinpoint the causes of sickness in a society, and to point to an alternative way of living. If followed, this will lead to a better and happier future; if not, society will reap a bitter harvest from the present situation. Prophecy thus points not only to problems but also to the possibilities of the present moment. This should not surprise us, for future hope is generally inseparable from honesty about the present.

Writing in Britain in the late 1980s it is difficult to feel much sense of hope, or vision, for the future. This is more than a personal impression; in Chapter 1 I cited Clodovis

Boff's comments about Europe, and to those I can add Lesslie Newbigin's observation that what he found most difficult about returning to Britain after nearly forty years in India was moving from a society that had much hope to one that had little.[17] Of course we might want to qualify such critical judgments. We might say, rightly, that events like Band Aid and Live Aid, and generous public response to appeals after disasters in places like Bangladesh and Armenia, point to people who are concerned for the world. However, such developments tend to be one-off events which do not challenge the structures of the northern hemisphere nations. In general we feel mired in an ambiguous heritage from the past, with little sense of what the way forward is going to be.

In finding our way forward we need to discover how to speak and live prophetically. There will be no sense of vision of the future unless we can put our finger on the ills of society, and see where and how alternative ways of living can be forged in the present. But insight and fresh vision inevitably depend on our ability to free ourselves from the prejudices and stereotypes that we have inherited, along with everyone else. Merton believed that silence and solitude could play a crucial role in this respect. For example, once, in the middle of the shopping district in Louisville, Kentucky, he had what for want of better words we must call a mystical experience. There 'at the corner of Fourth and Walnut' he was 'suddenly overwhelmed with realization that I loved all those people, that they were mine and I theirs, that we could not be alien to one another even though we were total strangers. It was like waking from a dream of separateness.'[18] In that ordinary, everyday, unremarkable setting he suddenly saw and felt God's love for each person, and the deep solidarity that existed between each member of the human race despite their illusions of separateness. It was a unity with each other that, if only they themselves could see it, would banish war, hatred, cruelty and greed. Reflecting on the experience afterwards, Merton linked it with his solitude and silence, feeling that these had made it possible for him to have this experience. And he added that it was impossible for people to have such

experiences if they were completely immersed in the 'cares
. . . illusions, and all the automatisms of a tightly collective
existence'.[19] He is referring to the way we constantly reinforce
one another's prejudices and false perceptions – of, for example, people of another race or class or country – a reinforce-
ment that is often unconscious. Listen to the anti-Irish jokes
in Britain and you will see what I mean.

This experience in Louisville proved to be a turning-point
in Merton's life, one that sustained and helped him in his
often controversial work for peace. Sometimes attempts were
made to silence him, for his anti-war writings had a powerful
impact. At one point his superiors forbade him to write for
publication on the topic. But always he was drawn on, encouraged in part by this vision of the nobility of each person and
their unity in God. His belief that the experience was made
possible by his solitude and silence points us towards a similar
lesson as we search for a spirituality that enables social action.
This is not, of course, to say that we too will have a mystical
vision if we practise stillness in solitude. But certainly Merton
believed that silence and solitude nourish a special prophetic
insight, and thus empower a person for justice and peace
work. The key lies in Merton's statement that solitude can
overcome the illusions and automatic responses of a tightly
collective existence. He is reminding us, I think, that the
contemplative focus on God draws a person's heart and mind
beyond the boundaries set around that person by the language
and concepts approved in society. To know God in silent
love is temporarily to disengage from the limitations and
distortions of society. This in turn allows a critical distance
to develop between oneself and the society of which one is
part. Shortly before his death by accidental electrocution in
Bangkok in 1968, Merton returned to this subject, and wrote
that 'The contemplative life must provide an area, a space of
liberty, of silence, in which possibilities are allowed to surface
and new choices – beyond routine choice – become manifest.
It should create a new experience of time . . . rooted in the
sense of common illusion and in criticism of it.'[20]

This is clearly important for any personal spirituality that would seek to engage with the need for change in society. Merton is *not* saying that contemplative prayer draws a person away from the world. He is saying that contemplative prayer draws a person away from the delusions with which people feed one another in society. These are general human delusions about self-sufficiency, about power in the sense of domination; they are the delusions of stereotypes and harmful myths, about ourselves and about other people.

Hence the paradox about being on the margins, which Merton saw as the proper place for the monk. Prayer in silence and solitude leads us for a time to the margins of society, and there, because we have created the space in our consciousness, we gain a greater ability to see into the heart of society. Contemplative prayer may thus involve conflict, as the lover of God is drawn from the security of the known, from the received wisdom of society, into the void of the unknown. But contemplative prayer also involves creativity, for the loving heart fixed on God in silence is freed to go beyond the conventions of what can be thought. Silence and solitude can thus be powerful enablers of the spark in the soul, of our dual love of God and the world as made and loved by God, who draws us away from its delusions so as to lead us deeper into its reality.

We live in an overwhelmingly verbal culture, in which there is a strong tendency to believe that better understanding depends on more words. But our very obsession with words derives from our culture's belief that we can dominate and control every aspect of reality around us. With words and prior concepts we project an analytical understanding on to the world, rather than allowing the world to disclose itself to us. We need more than ever to know that better understanding sometimes depends not on words but on silence. Merton himself once referred to 'the constant flood of language that pours meaninglessly over everybody, everywhere, from morning to night'. And he added that 'For language to have meaning, there must be intervals of silence somewhere, to divide word from word and utterance from utterance.'[21]

Perhaps there is an analogy here with learning another

language. It is a natural temptation to think that the skill of learning a new language lies in acquiring a good vocabulary, studying the grammar and mastering the pronunciation. Yet it is silence which is the secret in acquiring a new language, the silence in which we absorb not just the colloquialisms but the rhythms, the delicacies and the emotional resonances of the language being spoken around us. To learn a language well we have to see and feel from inside the world of those for whom it is their native tongue. This often requires a humble silence, in which we set self aside the better to enter into the world of others.[22] If we are to work for justice and peace, then we cannot escape the challenge to prophecy, which in turn requires us to enter into the heart of a society, to see its reality for what it is. Prophecy asks of us a preparedness to turn aside from the distractions and easy distortions of society, to seek the truth by seeking God who will send us back into society with a clearer vision. This is part of the dynamism of the spark in the soul. We learn to speak through silence; we learn to relate through solitude. Both of these help us to go beyond the conventions of our time and place.

Certainly Merton's own understanding of society became more penetrating as he grew within the silence that he experienced at Gethsemani, especially after he moved into the solitude of the hermitage there. In this sense he exemplifies all that he writes about with regard to how silence helps us see through surface appearances to the reality of the world. For example, in the late 1940s and early 1950s Merton was a comparatively uncritical citizen of the United States. These were of course the Cold War years. There is a particularly purple passage in *The Seven Storey Mountain* where he refers to the hidden life of prayer at Gethsemani Abbey as conferring a blessing on the USA. He intones:

> this church, this court of the Queen of Heaven, is the real capital of the country in which we are living. This is the center of all the vitality that is in America... These men, hidden in the anonymity of their choir and their white cowls, are doing for their land what no army, no congress,

no president could ever do as such: they are winning for it the grace and the protection and the friendship of God.[23]

Twenty years later he has something very different to say. He concludes then that the God worshipped by many Christians in the United States is a God made in their own image: a comfortable God, whose duty it is to account 'for the blessings that they enjoy in perpetuity'.[24] His sharp eye and sardonic pen note many delusions around him. He writes in his journal: 'At the moment everyone is talking about fallout shelters. (Build one in your backyard, come out after two weeks and resume the American Way of Life amid the ashes).'[25] He also notes that a letter arrives for him with the slogan, 'The US Army, key to peace'. He comments:

> No army is the key to peace, neither the US Army nor the Soviet Army nor any other. No 'great' nation has the key to anything but war. Power has nothing to do with peace. The more men build up military power, the more they violate peace and destroy it.[26]

Merton also wrote long, serious and hard-hitting pieces about the debasement of language and the consequences of this in national policy. Outstanding here is his essay 'War and the Crisis of Language' in which he ponders 'a classic example of the contamination of reason by speech, a statement by a US army major in Vietnam who said that it had been necessary to destroy a town in order to save it'. After analysing the self-enclosed, logical bizarreness of this statement, Merton concludes:

> The advantages of this kind of logic are no exclusive possession of the United States. This is purely and simply the logic shared by all war-makers. It is the logic of *power*. Possibly American generals are naïve enough to push this logic, without realizing, to absurd conclusions. But all who love power tend to think in some such way. Remember Hitler weeping over the ruins of Warsaw after it had been

demolished by the Luftwaffe: 'How wicked these people must have been,' he sobbed, 'to make me do this to them.'[27]

One wonders what Merton's comments would be today about United States policy in Central America.

I am not suggesting, of course, that we will all acquire the acuteness of vision of Thomas Merton if we arrange our lives so that there is space for silence and, if possible, solitude also. But I am saying (as he did himself) that in an age of a torrent of words, facts and theories we will be more open to clarity of understanding if we do provide space for silence and solitude. Such space allows the Holy Spirit to make its enlightening influence felt. It also allows us the emotional distance with which to separate good explanations from bad, true reasoning from false, history from propaganda. To nourish the spark in our soul there needs to be time for retreat, space to be prayerfully alone.

The contemplative approach

Contemplation tends to have a bad popular image. It is sometimes criticized as a form of prayer which draws people to God at the expense of their concern for the world. It is also thought of as a spirituality which encourages passivity.[28] I would disagree with both these interpretations. Thomas Merton is a clear example of someone who combined a love for contemplative prayer and a deep concern for justice and peace. In fact we can fully understand what Merton has to offer us for a spirituality of social action only if we take seriously his contemplative approach.

To see why this is so, it might be helpful to begin with Merton's criticisms of the spirit of our times. He sees western thinking as dominated by an instrumental approach to the world. Consciously or unconsciously, we tend to look at our surroundings with the implicit question in our minds, 'What is this *for*?' This flow of thought becomes so pervasive in our minds that we apply it not only to objects but to persons. We begin to think of other people as significant only if useful – and of course ourselves also. Merton comments: 'As a result, men are valued not for what they are but for what they do or what they have – for their usefulness.'[29] Thus Merton complains that in contemporary western culture, 'Nothing is allowed just to be and to mean itself. . .' Instead everything is viewed in terms of its practical use, as a means to an end.[30] This is one of the ways that Merton interprets the Christian myth of the Fall, as referring to the development of a human desire to exploit people and things in the interests of pleasure and power. And, he adds, the almost absolute power to manipulate the world given by technology has made this human condition more obvious than ever – witness, he says, the horror of extermination camps and nuclear weapons. The problem lies in 'man's own technocratic and self-centred "worldliness" which . . . enables him to act out his fantasies as a little autonomous god, seeing everything in relation to himself'.[31] Here Merton sounds like Eckhart, who, as we saw in Chapter 3, encouraged detachment as one way of overcoming this tendency to re-order the world around ourselves and our desires.

But is Merton right? We might want to demur. The plain fact is that the spirit of technological and scientific inquiry has greatly enhanced the quality of human life. I remember going around the medical museum at Guy's Hospital in London. There you can see what an operating theatre used to look like in the days before anaesthetics, complete with straps to restrain the patient. There is also a cabinet with shelves lined in green baize, on which the instruments rested after each operation; the museum's own notes draw attention to how this would have created a terrible source of infection. Those days are gone, thanks to the ceaselessly inquiring human mind, and none of us would want them back.

However I think that Merton is drawing our attention to a genuine problem of our present western culture. Merton does overbalance in his attacks on it, but we ought to focus on the direction his criticism leads us. For Merton is reminding us that the human mind which grasps facts and insights is only able to operate safely if it is itself drawn into God – which is one way of understanding contemplative prayer.

This is why Merton stresses that a Christian respect for the world must proceed from a grateful contemplative awareness of all being as deriving from God, who sustains not only the world but also each person in his or her identity. In contemplative prayer we enter into this awareness, discovering God not as a 'fact' over against ourselves, but in the deepest ground of our being, present to us always in love. Merton frequently refers to this intuition or awareness of God, who eludes the categorizing mind but reveals himself to us in the experience of love. The following passage from *Contemplative Prayer* probably sums up Merton on this point:

> God is invisibly present to the ground of our being: our belief and love attain to him, but he remains hidden from the arrogant gaze of our investigating mind which seeks to capture him and secure permanent possession of him in an act of knowledge that gives *power over him*. It is in fact absurd and impossible to try and grasp God as an object which can be seized and comprehended by our minds. . . Instead we know him in so far as we become aware of ourselves as known through and through by him. We 'possess' him in proportion as we realize ourselves to be possessed by him in the inmost depths of our being.[32]

Knowing God is thus a knowing of ourselves and our whole world as utterly dependent on him. It is also – and here Merton is faithful to the whole mystical tradition – a form of knowledge that requires us to set aside all our previous understanding of what it means to know. In knowing God we do not know through our senses, through concepts, through the intellect or even in any ordinary sense through the emotions. Rather, 'One knows God by becoming one with Him. One apprehends him by becoming the object of His infinite mercies.'[33]

Contemplative prayer thus has the effect of overcoming the temptation to see ourselves as isolated observers, looking out on our world to judge it, assess it, dominate and use it. It replaces this with a growing consciousness of ourselves as found by God. We are no longer the ultimate judge of all that we see, assessing it in terms of usefulness. Instead we are confronted by the all-embracing reality of God who – as we noted from Gutierrez in Chapter 4 – goes beyond the language of usefulness and uselessness. The point I am trying to make here is that we sail through so much of daily life establishing ourselves in the world, making our influence felt, operating according to norms and practices that we have inherited from others. In contemplative prayer we slowly learn to change our focus. We are drawn into what is infinitely greater than ourselves, and find that ultimate reality, ultimate truth are not found by self-assertion. Rather they are given to us as we learn to let go and stop 'making' our world. We begin to learn to see from another perspective, in which we are not at the centre of the universe; we begin to learn to wait. Because we are no longer the busy centre of the world, we grow in the capacity really to hear what other people are saying, and we become better able to judge what an appropriate response by us would be to different situations that challenge us. This is because we have learned, through contemplative prayer, to cease projecting ourselves on to the world, with all our anxieties and aggressions, and begun to see people and things as they truly are. Finally contemplative prayer reveals to us God beyond definition and God beyond images; it therefore brings us up against the utter reality of God, who challenges our safe assumptions and our traditional roles. To discover God beyond any encapsulation is to find that our ritual responses about goodness and love are not satisfactory. God who is beyond us and ahead of us calls us on to a newer understanding of what Christian living should be like.

For all these reasons, the contemplative experience tends to convert those who enter into it. It is a radicalizing experience. Merton wrote that genuine contemplation challenges any stale goodness with which people operate, goodness which is content with established procedures and safe formulas: 'Such "goodness" is preserved by routine and the habitual avoidance of serious risk – indeed of serious challenge . . . while turning a blind eye to the greatest enormities of injustice and uncharity.'[34] Contemplative love of God pulls people out of their comfortable rut. It makes them reject formulas which explain away the plight of the poor or which dismiss the clouds of war. God's uncompromising love shows up human compromises; it illuminates and throws into sharp relief the standards we judge by, and this is true both for those who have previously been committed to social justice and those who have not. This, I think, is why Merton says that the more we love God the more we will become disturbing people. He is scathing about those who try to become 'well-adjusted' members of society. He calls it the road to servility and shallowness, and says that we become fulfilled to the extent that we follow Christ's unconditional 'Yes' to God.[35] In prayer, after all, we seek an experience of God's love and mercy, and intend to live what we experience:

> But my life and aims tend to be artificial, inauthentic, as long as I am simply trying to adjust my actions to certain exterior norms of conduct that will enable me to play an approved part in the society in which I live. After all, this amounts to little more than learning a *role*.[36]

If we move into contemplative prayer then we can expect to find that our whole outlook is being reshaped. This experience is not a recipe for conformism. On the contrary, it can make us sensitive to the truth about society, and it can make us aware of the right way to live (as opposed to the conventional way of behaving). This is a lesson that we noted with regard to Eckhart, that by learning to leave behind a superficial self-image and discovering who we really are before God, we discover the freedom to act out of what we really know to be true.

This is why contemplative prayer provides energy and strength in the ceaseless struggle for a just society. Action for justice and peace becomes less and less a case of obedience to external norms, and more a case of responding to one's deepest intuitions and desires. This has the effect of helping prevent the exhaustion and 'compassion burnout' that can come from guilt, which I mentioned in Chapter 1. Contemplative prayer is mystical in that it is an entering into the realm of divine reality; a person feels a wordless exchange of love with God. Moreover this experience of God's love and holiness, though beyond conceptual formulation, affects all of a person's perceptions of the world. It allows an entry into something of God's love for humankind and for nature – a process dramatically symbolized, as we saw in Chapter 2, with the giving of the stigmata to Francis. On the one hand this sharing of the divine perspective tends to create a holistic understanding of the natural order, which helps us to respect it (and is thus the opposite of the exploitative instrumentalism so loathed by Merton). On the other hand it helps us to seek the removal from society of all that pains God, in a longing that comes from deep inside us. This is because it is a spontaneous desire arising out of the person's own experience of God, analogous to the inner development which we saw described by Eckhart as the birth of the Word in the soul.

What though, about the criticism that this sort of contemplative experience is reserved for a spiritual élite? Certainly there are mountains of mystical prayer which few are privileged to climb. However, many more of us find ourselves on the foothills than realize the fact. There are times in prayer when we find that our words cease and our thoughts are stilled. They are, curiously enough, sometimes moments of heightened perception: we may be aware of footsteps on the pavement outside, of the distant wail of a police siren, of the children playing next door. But these sounds will be drawn into the deeper silence within us, into that pool of silence in our hearts where the Spirit leads us to God. It is then that, all too briefly, we know ourselves completely loved and accepted, drawn into the depths of God's embrace.

Contemplative prayer is not a kind of esoteric science, available to a few people only, but a capacity which could and should be developed by many people in different walks of life. Merton believed that it could fit into the life of any

114

person attracted to it.[37] In fact he recommended that ordinary Christians take seriously the *necessity* of pursuing contemplative prayer, including the disciplines necessary to allow it to flourish – being open to God in prayer, persevering in silence and inner stillness, setting aside thoughts and ideas to allow a simple desire for God to carry us forward. He felt that 'in the pressures of modern urban life, many will feel the need for a certain interior silence and discipline simply to keep themselves together, to maintain their human and Christian identity and their spiritual freedom'.[38]

Freedom is both the goal and the source that Merton points us towards in our search for a personal spirituality which can undergird a Christian commitment to social action. It is freedom, first, that comes from finding God within our own depths, God as the creator and guardian of our identity. Secondly freedom is the outcome of creating space for silence and solitude in our lives, allowing us to know the Spirit's guidance which will take us through and beyond society's distortions and prejudices, helping us towards a prophetic insight. Finally freedom is God's gift when God draws us into contemplative prayer, helping us leave ourselves and our narrow world-views behind, to discover a new centre out of which we can live within the dynamism of God's own love for the world – which becomes the spark in our soul.

1 Monica Furlong, *Merton: a biography* (New York, 1980), p. 161.
2 Thomas Merton, *Conjectures of a Guilty Bystander* (New York, 1968), p. 49.
3 J. F. Teahan, 'The Place of Silence in Thomas Merton's Life and Thought', in Patrick Hart (ed.), *The Message of Thomas Merton* (Kalamazoo, Michigan, 1981), p. 94.
4 Michael Mott, *The Seven Mountains of Thomas Merton* (Boston, 1984), p. 487. The first volume of his letters, edited by William Shannon, is published as *The Hidden Ground of Love* (New York, 1985).
5 Thomas Merton, *The Sign of Jonas* (London, 1953), p. 11.
6 See article by Teahan, cited above, for a fine treatment of this tension in Merton.
7 Mott, op. cit., pp. 317–18, 438.
8 *Conjectures of a Guilty Bystander*, p. 150.

9 Thomas Merton, *Zen and the Birds of Appetite* (New York, 1968), p. 31.
10 *Conjectures of a Guilty Bystander*, p. 224.
11 ibid., p. 75.
12 *Zen and the Birds of Appetite*, p. 15.
13 *Conjectures of a Guilty Bystander*, p. 86.
14 *Zen and the Birds of Appetite*, pp. 11–12.
15 ibid., p. 24.
16 Thomas Merton, *New Seeds of Contemplation* (London, 1964), p. 105.
17 Lesslie Newbigin, *The Other Side of 1984* (Geneva, 1983), p. 1.
18 *Conjectures of a Guilty Bystander*, p. 156.
19 ibid., p. 158.
20 Thomas Merton, *Asian Journal* (London, 1974), p. 117.
21 Thomas Merton, *The Monastic Journey* (London, 1977), pp. 153–4.
22 See Ivan Illich, *Celebration of Awareness* (London, 1973), pp. 39–46, for a meditation on the role of silence in learning a language.
23 Thomas Merton, *The Seven Storey Mountain* (London, 1975), p. 325.
24 Thomas Merton, *Faith and Violence* (Notre Dame, Ind., 1968).
25 *Conjectures of a Guilty Bystander*, p. 191.
26 ibid., p. 41.
27 Thomas Merton, *On Peace* (London, 1976), p. 143.
28 See for instance the strictures of Matthew Fox in *A Spirituality Named Compassion* (Minneapolis, 1979), chs 1, 2.
29 *Conjectures of a Guilty Bystander*, p. 308.
30 *Zen and the Birds of Appetite*, p. 30.
31 *Conjectures of a Guilty Bystander*, p. 294.
32 Thomas Merton, *Contemplative Prayer* (London, 1972), p. 103.
33 Thomas Merton, 'The Inner Experience: infused contemplation' in *Cistercian Studies*, vol. 19, no. 1 (1984), p. 63 (art. ed. Patrick Hart).
34 *Contemplative Prayer*, p. 130.
35 *Conjectures of a Guilty Bystander*, pp. 264–8.
36 *Contemplative Prayer*, pp. 84–5.
37 ibid., p. 33.
38 ibid., p. 20.

6

Towards a Spirituality of Resistance

It would be a counsel of perfection to try and integrate the insights of the four mystics I have looked at. It would also be impossible. Even my metaphor of the spark in the soul has been only a very loosely defined element. Despite this feature in all four, some important differences can be found. The greatest difference is probably between Francis of Assisi and Meister Eckhart. Francis is strongly Christ-centred, and is drawn into God by the power of images. Eckhart says little about the historical Jesus, and approaches God through detachment, including detachment from images. In this respect Francis and Eckhart represent two basic streams in Christian spirituality. Which of these two approaches to adopt will vary from person to person. Some may be drawn to one of these ways at one stage in life, and to another at a later stage. Much work has also been done recently in spirituality which has shown that different spiritualities will appeal to different personality types.[1] In finding a personal spirituality which draws us into social action we need to remember that there are various ways in, and that not everyone benefits from the same approach.

There is, however, one feature which stands out in each of the four mystics we have looked at. I refer to their preparedness to challenge the socially approved understanding of correct and proper behaviour; their willingness to leave behind the norms and conventions of their day, in order to be obedient to God. Francis, for example, left his family home in the social and geographical centre of Assisi to live with lepers – on the social and geographical margin. 'Decent places' is how

117

a thirteenth-century biographer of Francis defiantly refers to the homes of such people. Even the criminal underworld of the forests was to be befriended. Francis found 'his own side', the Crusaders, to be dissolute; he visited the arch-enemy the Sultan, who entered into dialogue and treated him with respect. We know much less about Meister Eckhart, but enough to note the care he gave to communities of women, and the respect he showed for their intellectual capacity. There is also the interesting feature of his preaching in the vernacular, encouraging people in an age of ornate religious practice not to worry about external obligations, and to seek God within them. Like Francis, we have in Eckhart someone prepared to go against the grain of conventional wisdom and to challenge social assumptions. In so doing he exposed himself to a charge of heresy.

Evelyn Underhill could have been content with the social round of a barrister's wife. Despite increasingly debilitating attacks of asthma she pursued a punishing schedule of lecturing, writing, counselling and retreat-giving. More remarkably she became increasingly concerned about issues such as urban poverty, racism and militarism, and used her influence to try and persuade people in Britain to tackle these urgent issues. Finally, like Francis of Assisi, she detached herself from the opinions of people around her and promoted non-violence as part of Christian faith. Thomas Merton saw through the pious clichés of American patriotism, and called his fellow-citizens to a truer obedience. He exposed how their image of God had been accommodated to American cultural norms. Merton contrasted this faith with discovery of God in contemplative prayer, a God who challenges our assumptions and breaks down our self-centred, exploitative world-view, to lead us into true wisdom. His own experiences made Merton a powerful prophet, frequently exposing the lies and half-truths that were used to justify policies like the Vietnam war. He went out of his way to encourage groups and individuals who were opposed to war and injustice.

When we look back at our four mystics in this way, their courage and unconventionality seem remarkable. Their witness seems to have emerged out of a combination of a deep personal spirituality and radical openness to society. Put slightly differently, they were integrating their experiences of the world into their prayer life and their prayer into their experience of the world. Francis loved the Eucharist, and praised God through the beauty of creation; he was also acutely aware of the sufferings of the poor and of the horror of war. Eckhart was elected by his brethren to high office, and so we may conjecture that he did not neglect his religious duties – indeed the existence of transcribed sermons shows that he prepared carefully for preaching, and must of course have been frequently at mass, sometimes as celebrant. He was also able to see the intellectual potential of women and of ordinary folk in general, at a time when the church was extremely chauvinist and hierarchical. Underhill went to mass and confession regularly, and was under a spiritual director for twenty years. Yet she recognized the truth about slums in Britain's divided society of the 1920s and 1930s, and became aware of the truth about war. Merton was strongly committed to prayer, initially to the sevenfold office and meditation times in the abbey at Gethsemani, later in his hermitage.[2] But he was also listening to the voices of the world. He knew by reading and correspondence and visitors what was going on not only in the ghettos of US cities but also in Latin America and South-East Asia.

In each of these four we seem to find the spark in the soul, in the sense of a reciprocity between their personal spirituality and their awareness of the world. In each of them there seems also to come a point in which they have the courage to go beyond the safe and the approved. Their movement into God has brought them to a place of insight and they cannot keep silent. But their commitment in this way remains none the less courageous and moving. Sometimes they risked the wrath of authority. Sometimes they were exposed to something perhaps even harder to bear, the mocking scorn of others. I labour this point because it seems to have particular relevance today. It is frequently said that there is renewed interest in spirituality, which is certainly true. But not all of this interest is necessarily 'earthed' in reality. There is, I suspect, a temptation when we cannot change the exterior world to retreat to the interior world which we feel is under our control. And so there is a danger that people will unconsciously turn to spirituality because they feel that they can contribute nothing to change society. But the four mystics we have looked at in this book remind us that one test of a healthy spirituality is whether or not it leads us to a place where we are prepared to part company with the easy assumptions and misleading wisdom of those around us. I would suggest therefore that if we are prepared to take spirituality seriously then we should ask ourselves if we are willing to risk scorn or ridicule, to stand out rather than to stand back. It is a question of whether we are prepared, where necessary, to refuse to conform, to let our faith lead us into a spirituality of resistance to false norms. Christians who participate in justice and peace movements usually are so prepared. If the current interest in spirituality is healthy and well-founded, then presumably we can expect many other Christians to join them.

Yet the four mystics we have looked at have a question too, precisely for Christians who are already committed to social action. It is a question about whether they are prepared to undertake the humdrum routine task of spiritual discipline: regular prayer, silence and solitude, love of the Eucharist, and receiving spiritual direction. Traditional sources of renewal such as these seem to have greatly strengthened the four whom we have looked at. Now, people active for social change do sometimes show a real degree of asceticism. Those who take ecology seriously, for instance, embrace a simple lifestyle that I and others continue to learn from; in this sense they are creating an asceticism for our times. But perhaps more traditional forms of asceticism are important too, when it comes to constructing a spirituality for social action. This point is made by Grace Jantzen, who notes that we find in all of the outstanding figures of English spirituality:

in one form or another the practice of radical renunciation of the things that blind: because they rooted out the lust for power in themselves, they were able to see the corruption of power and its effect on the oppressed; because they rejected greed, they could see the poor; because their quest for knowledge was not anchored in ambition or desire to impress they could teach the ignorant. Their vision of God, their vision of the needs of the world, their perception of the corrupt structures that prevented those needs from being met were undistorted by personal entanglement with position or power or wealth: it is this, I think, that makes them *spiritual* giants.[3]

Although she does not use the phrase, I think it fair to say that Jantzen concludes that their asceticism led these men and women into what was, in their own day and own way, a spirituality of resistance. This points to the importance of a sustained personal discipline as a means of opening our eyes and sustaining our ability to commit ourselves to social action. Our four mystics showed precisely such a discipline, and were greatly enabled by it.

It is worth remembering at this point that some of the great men and women of prayer were people of amazing stamina and energy. Catherine of Genoa created a system of hospitals to serve the poorest people of her fifteenth-century city. John of the Cross withstood solitary confinement and whippings designed to break his spirit, and went on to become a reformer of his order. Teresa of Avila defied the limitations on the role of women and nuns in Spain of her day, to range across the country in a bullock cart establishing convents. John Woolman, eighteenth-century American Quaker, campaigned vigorously against slavery. Arthur Shearly Cripps, Anglican priest, worked tirelessly in colonial Rhodesia to defend African peasant farmers from government attempts to confiscate their land for white farmers. (He walked hundreds of miles rather than rush past the poor in a car, leaving them in a shower of dust.) Evelyn Underhill was fascinated by the energizing aspect of prayer, and encouraged those she taught to expect it for themselves. She wrote, 'History . . . shows us, again and again, that men and women of prayer tap a source

of energy, possess a tranquil courage, an initiative, a faith.'[4]
If as Christians we go for action without contemplation, for
commitment without prayer, we may actually be short-
changing ourselves and diminishing our energy and resolve.

There is, however, at least one major difference between
the times of the first three of our mystics and our own times.
The late-twentieth-century world is a world of a ceaseless flow
of information. News both urgent and banal bombards us all
the time. The telecommunications revolution brings us images
from the farthest corners of the globe. As I pointed out in
Chapter 4, great efforts are expended by powerful people and
institutions to bring before us the images and impressions
which they want us to see. Even if we do not live in a
dictatorship or totalitarian society there is a real, if subtle
effort made to control what we perceive and think. Against
this background it becomes difficult sometimes to hear the
poor or suffering people speak for themselves; it becomes
difficult to see how our own country or class contributes to
other people's suffering. To this has to be added another
problem flowing from the communications revolution, the
trivialization of the news. In Britain there has been a retreat
into fantasy, with the personages of television drama series
being elevated to the status of major news events. A bizarre
reversal of values has taken place, in which fictional charac-
ters are more real than people caught up in – for example –
famine or torture.

For both these reasons, the communications revolution
challenges us to create a spirituality of resistance in our own
times. From Merton we learned the importance of periods of
withdrawal, of entry into silence so as to be able to listen
with discernment. But when we are not in such a time and
space of silence and solitude, I would suggest that we are
required to be more questioning of the news, more vigilant
of what we see and hear, than any previous generation. In
Chapter 4 I mentioned listening to the poor and oppressed
as part of this process of sifting. Wherever possible we also
have to be asking 'Who profits?' from any development. And
wherever possible, we have to be prepared actively to watch

what is happening to the most vulnerable people around us. We need to be alert, and critically aware. When Primo Levi wrote about his horrifying concentration camp experiences, many people asked him whether or not the German people had been aware of what was going on in places like Auschwitz. Levi replied:

> In Hitler's Germany a particular code was widespread: those who knew did not talk; those who did not know did not ask questions; those who did ask questions received no answers. In this way the typical German citizen won and defended his ignorance. . . Shutting his mouth, his eyes and his ears, he built for himself the illusion of not knowing, hence not being an accomplice to the things taking place in front of his very door.[5]

Although his words are a condemnation of a particular people at a particular time and place, Levi is describing a mechanism of denial that operates in many other circumstances. Unless we are prepared to be vigilant, unless we are prepared to resist the tidal wave of news trivia, we can end up being as complicit as those Germans who refused to ask questions, who denied the evidence that they saw and heard, and thought it was always somebody else's responsibility. In this sense there is a pressing need for a spirituality of resistance.

Finally, if we build such a spirituality, it will need to be one of patient faith that is prepared for the long haul. If we seek social action out of our love of God then we need to accept that we may never see the fruit of the seeds that we sow, believing that others will reap it. Jim Douglass has founded a community of peace witnesses next to a Trident submarine base in Washington State in the United States. He treasures a t-shirt someone gave him with the words 'Patience is a revolutionary virtue'. That patient staying-power – what the New Testament calls *hypomene* – is the bedrock of any spirituality for social action. Our times of prayer and openness to God, our solidarity with the poor, our silence and solitude, our preparedness to listen and question, our struggle for detachment and discipline – these may seem fragile tools with which to commit ourselves to social action. But as we saw from the four mystics we have studied, these tools, along with patience, can be revolutionary virtues.

1 See for example Christopher Bryant, *The Heart in Pilgrimage* (London, 1980), pp. 182–95; Chester P. Michael and Marie C. Norrissey, *Prayer and Temperament* (Charlotteville, Va., 1984).
2 Descriptions of Merton's praying can be found in Thomas P. McDonnell (ed.), *A Thomas Merton Reader*, rev. edn (New York, 1974), pp. 433–4; and in Merton's letter to Abdul Aziz in William Shannon (ed.), *The Hidden Ground of Love* (New York, 1985), pp. 63–4. Merton also refers to saying his office and celebrating mass on his trip to Asia in *Asian Journal*.
3 Grace Jantzen, *English Spirituality*, Address to the Nikaean Club (privately printed), p. 7.
4 Evelyn Underhill, *Mixed Pasture* (London, 1933), p. 73.
5 Primo Levi, *If This is a Man* and *The Truce* (London, 1987), p. 386.